The Prophet

Khalil Gibran

English & Arabic

Jamil Elabed

8th edition (Golden Copy)

ISBN: 978-0-9928995-2-3 (Paperback)
          978-0-9928995-3-0 (Hardback)
          978-0-9928995-4-7 (ePub)

British Library Catalogue-in-Publication Data

A catalogue record of the print edition is available from the British Library

Cover artwork by **Glenn D Webster**

*This 8th edition of the translation, earmarked "**The Golden Copy**," is the final version of the translation that supersedes all the previous seven versions thereof.*

The images in this translation are more accurately defined, more intellectually oriented and more intense than those in Gibran's texts. Butrous Hallaq, critic and professor of Arabic Literature, Sorbonne University, Paris, France.

This translation conveys the sheerness and diaphaneity of Gibran's spirit. Had Gibran written The Prophet in Arabic, he would have done what Jamil Elabed has done with his masterly pen. Sabah Kabbani, Syrian writer, artist and diplomat.

I return to The Prophet in Jamil Elabed's translation to find it deeper and more graceful than my knowledge of it from previous translations. Abdessalaam Al-Ojaily, Syrian foreign minister, parliamentarian, physician and novelist.

This elegant work reveals the translator's wide knowledge, ability and resourcefulness. Riad Nourallah, professor of translation, Westminster University, London, UK.

Dazzling, spellbinding and enchanting. Lebanese daily Al-Safeer.

This translation feels like an original work. It captures all the dimensions of Gibran, even those the English language in which he wrote did not help him convey. Zuhair Samhouri, English philology professor, Damascus University, Syria.

One cannot tell with any certainty who wrote the Arabic and who wrote the English. Muhammad Kujjah, president of Syria's Archaeological Society.

This is a transcendental ladder to the clouds and a window unto the stars. I hope to see it turned into a musical, for every word in it bursts with melody and awakens the spirit. Rafiq Al-Sabban, Syrian film director and script writer.

This translation preserved the glow akin to Gibran's visions. Hanna Mineh, Syrian novelist.

An elevated translation of the highest quality. Ragheed Al-Solh, Oxford University, UK.

*

Jamil Elabed is a Syrian-British translator who worked as a broadcast journalist at the BBC World Service in 1994 and in the spring of 1998 published the first edition of his translation of Gibran's The Prophet. He won the European Union Commission's Creative Translation Award followed by the British University of East Anglia's Translation Residency Grant. He has been a full member of the Institute of Translation and Interpreting (ITI) since 2000. Jamil has taught translation and interpreting at Leeds University while freelancing as a professional conference interpreter.

The Golden Copy Edition

It has taken me twenty years and eight editions to bring my translation of Gibran's *The Prophet* into the author's mother tongue, Arabic, to what it is now.

Readers alone will decide whether I have done full justice to the English original. For to do less than that I am aware, is an unacceptable and unforgivable distortion of one of the most revered books in the history of man.

I have persevered because I wanted to provide Arabic-speaking readers the very same pleasure that readers of the original text have been experiencing for decades.

This *eighth* Golden Copy edition supersedes the previous seven editions of my translation of this masterpiece. It is my final refinement of my translation of the book that has changed my life, and for which I am forever grateful.

With love,

Jamil

Foreword

Khalil Gibran's visionary paths are remote and hard to discern, let alone comprehend. But we cannot afford to deny them. And what cannot be denied may not be ignored. We know for certain that what is here is not all that is there. And we should never stop seeking and searching and researching. The quest to unravel the mystery has long become second nature. And it is unstoppable.

Drawing on his vast imagination, Gibran sought the unknown. But it was not just his imagination. Nature equipped him with additional visionary tools to carry out the search. He harnessed the power of contemplation, which is the engine of the imagination. Contemplation and imagination pave the path to visions that conjure up inspiration. Nature, the womb of all things, meant that to happen in the heart and mind of the little man from *Bsharri*, Mount Lebanon, even as she instils more sugar in a cluster of grapes than in another cluster on the same bush.

Gibran's mighty imagination lent him wings to venture far, to where the grand spirit abides. Seeking the unknown is a realistic mission. Unravelling the mysteries of the unknown has forever been man's relentless dream. It is the very dream that NASA seeks to fulfil. The difference between NASA and Gibran is that the latter used different tools. He unleashed his powers of contemplation, imagination and insight to reach far and wide led by the silent knowledge of the heart that *knows the secrets of the days and the nights.* He was a realist in a visionary sense. He explored his heart's knowledge and gave it voice.

Nature breathed into him and he caught her breath in words. Nature touched his soul as it did no other man. And he would contemplate nature more than any other man has done. For nature has an ultimate dream. And her dream is for man to see and to hear.

But man all too often finds it hard to see the images behind the images and to hear the sounds behind the sounds. He is so overwhelmed with material concerns and with the day-to-day business of satisfying direct bodily needs. Yet the visions are always there to grasp. They are landmarks revisited. They are stops on the way to further visions while the mist crystallises and the formless takes form.

And when man contemplates nature, she responds. She returns the attention by bestowing inspiration. For nature wants to be known to her own children. Her heart forever yearns to theirs. *The Prophet* was nature's response to Gibran's addictive contemplation. Through the joy and ecstasy of her inspiration, she invited him to contemplate more. She always craves more attention to inspire more.

A distance crossed through contemplation, imagination and insight is a vision achieved, and visions are towers in the sky that man builds on the way to finding the truth. They are the stars that light up the darkness of man's inner and outer being.

Gibran saw through the mist that veils the truth. And what is the truth except a vision, an image of the infinite made visible through contemplation?

The soul that Gibran sought was the soul of all things, including man's soul. *The Prophet* is also Gibran's expedition to explore self. For self is infinite as space is

"Like the ocean is your god-self;
It remains forever undefiled.
And like the ether it lifts but the winged.
Even like the sun is your god-self;
It knows not the ways of the mole nor seeks it the holes
of the serpent.
But your god-self dwells not alone in your being.
Much in you is still man, and much in you is not yet
man,
But a shapeless pigmy that walks asleep in the mist
searching for its own awakening."

Every one of us seeks their own awakening. We walk at a different pace and stride and with different visions, but we are all on the same journey nonetheless.

In man's destined search for awakening lies his evolution from pigmy self to god-self. It is only in his awareness of the ugliness of the one and the holiness of the other that he is given the chance to turn to the good and away from the bad.

The body dies but visions never perish. They are treasured *in the sealed memory that keeps records of our yesteryears, while* man's *procession to the infinite* continues.

Man will forever seek the unknown that Kahlil Gibran sought despite the vagueness. He said in *The Prophet*:

"If these be vague words, then seek not to clear them.

Vague and nebulous is the beginning of all things, but not their end.

And I fain would have you remember me as a beginning.

Life and all that lives, is conceived in the mist and not in the crystal.

And who knows but a crystal is mist in decay?

This would I have you remember in remembering me:

That which seems most feeble and bewildered in you is the strongest and most determined.

Is not your breath that erected and hardened the structure of your bones?

And is not a dream which none of you remember having dreamt, that builded your city and fashioned all there is in it?

Could you but see the tides of that breath you would cease to see all else,

And if you could hear the whispering of the dream you

But you do not see, nor do you hear, and that is well.

The veil that clouds your eyes shall be lifted by the hands that wove it,

And the clay that fills your ears shall be pierced by those fingers that kneaded it.

And you shall see

And you shall hear.

Yet you shall not deplore having known blindness, nor regret having been deaf.

For in that day you shall know the hidden purposes in all things,

And you shall bless darkness as you would bless light."

Gibran's *The Prophet* is a pulsing record of life and of the conduct of nature for man to be one with life's melody; when life is a song we can all sing. Life's beauty is silent. Man's beauty is loud. When they match and blend together, the stars join in the festivity.

The Prophet is a landmark vision of man inspired by nature on the way to man's oneness with life. It is a song in praise of the beauty of life that manifests itself in the brook that runs unseen in the mountains, and in the cloud that carries life to the isolated myrtle.

But why Gibran? My answer is that not all of us walk the same paths. We use different routes and different trails and tools, though the aim is the same. Nature has scattered us about just like she scatters pollen to be selected randomly by the bee and from the bee to the anemone. Some of the pollen have more nectar glands than others. Nature bestows her gifts on men and women like raindrops on the adjacent field. Saturated with freshness of heart and clarity of vision, Gibran bore sweet fruit. He contemplated life and his winged imagination reached far. And when his soul was *heavy-laden with her own ripe fruit,* and when it *ran over with the wine of the ages,* he poured out the content of his heart for the parched souls.

Often, we query the existence of God, yet we refrain from disputing the power that keeps the galaxies in orbit. Gibran understood the realities of his visions before he ventured to tell us about them. And he talked with the confidence and faith of a man whose heart and mind had nothing in them but love. Gibran's visions tell us of the untold, of the unseen yet sensed, of the remote yet near, and of the vast yet small.

The Prophet has sold more than a hundred million copies

translated into more than forty languages they also say. However, it is the shadow of the truth in the book that has sold in such abundance; the decoded messages in this book that keep coming from the beyond.

We move with body and soul that are separable. But even the universe is also body and soul. The star that is rock and dust has a soul that blinks and inspires; the moon that is arid and empty offers volumes of poetry to man on earth; the seas, rivers, lakes and mountains whisper to one another in the stillness of the night, and each one of them sings their own song with life.

Inspiration is communication. Each kind communicates with their own kind. Whatever inspiration a man contemplating receives from the unknown is a message from man's own kind. However vague the message, further contemplation will decode the message. For one kind is destined to decipher what comes from its own kind.

The hours man spends contemplating the leaves enchanted under the setting sun is telling evidence of the communication between man and nature. All that receive moon that receives light inspires the heart, provokes the mind, and makes merry with the tide; the roots that receive water in the heart of the earth give life to the earth; and the lowlands receive from the highlands and give to the fields. And man, who receives from all, gives to all. He is the one who hunts the visions which release the soul to soar high in the sky.

The Prophet is a March of Triumph for man's larger self; a resurrection of what has remained dormant since man's appearance on the blue globe; a transcendental road map and a spiritual strategy to enable man's larger self to prevail; a magnifying glass pinpointing the otherwise unnoticed qualities that are deeply rooted in man.

Life has the coffers of her bounty open at all times to those who care to receive, but few take. She has all her fountains *overrunning with the wine of the ages* at all times, but few drink.

Gibran's words were not ordinary words and his visions were not ordinary visions. They were cast by his kind heart and moulded by his awakened soul. They were from a reservoir entirely his own.

When Gibran dared the distances, he aimed for the truth, knowing that more towers still need to be built and more visions still need to be reached before a glimpse of the truth can be revealed.

Man's journey to the unknown will continue. Even the sightless walk the same wondrous routes and experience the same unforetold discoveries and awe, while the questions flow and the answers abound.

Reading and rereading *The Prophet* invokes and revives the process of spiritual evolution that nature has availed to man, bringing us closer and closer to *the holy mountain*.

Jamil Elabed

For Katrina and Ryan

Contents

The Prophet

ALMUSTAFA, the chosen and the beloved, who was a dawn upon his own day, had waited twelve years in the city of Orphalese for his ship that was to return and bear him back to the isle of his birth.

And in the twelfth year, on the seventh day of Ielool, the month of reaping, he climbed the hill without the city walls and looked seaward; and he beheld his ship coming with the mist.

Then the gates of his heart were flung open, and his joy flew far over the sea. And he closed his eyes and prayed in the silences of his soul.

لبث المصطفى، المختار الحبيب، من كان فجراً طالعاً على زمانه، اثني عشر عاماً في مدينة أورفليس ينتظر سفينته التي ستحمله وتعود به إلى ربوع ميلاده.

وفي السنة الثانية عشرة، يوم السابع من أيلول، شهر القطاف، صعد التل وراء سور المدينة وولى بصره شطر البحر ؛ فرأى السفينة قادمة مع الضباب.

انفرجت أسارير قلبه وحلق بصره بعيداً فوق أديم الماء. ثم أغمض وصلى في سكنات روحه.

But as he descended the hill, a sadness came upon him, and he thought in his heart:

How shall I go in peace and without sorrow? Nay, not without a wound in the spirit shall I leave this city.

Long were the days of pain I have spent within its walls, and long were the nights of aloneness; and who can depart from his pain and his aloneness without regret?

Too many fragments of the spirit have I scattered in these streets, and too many are the children of my longing that walk naked among these hills, and I cannot withdraw from them without a burden and an ache.

It is not a garment I cast off this day, but a skin that I tear with my own hands.

وفيما هبط التل حلت عليه كآبة، وفكر في قلبه:

كيف أرحل بسلام وبلا أسى؟ لا، لن أبرح هذه المدينة من غير جرح يصيب روحي.

طويلة أيام الألم أمضيتها بين ظهرانيها، وطويلة ليالي الوحدة؛ وهل من يقدر على هجر وحدته وألمه من دون حسرة؟

كثيرة شظايا الروح نثرتها على هذه الطرقات، وكثيرة بنات شوقي تخطر عارية بين التلال، ولن أستطيع منها فكاكاً بدون وجع وأحمال.

ليس الأمر رداء أنزعه اليوم عني، بل لحم تمزقه يداي.

Nor is it a thought I leave behind me, but a heart made sweet with hunger and with thirst.

Yet I cannot tarry longer.

The sea that calls all things unto her calls me, and I must embark.

For to stay, though the hours burn in the night, is to freeze and crystallize and be bound in a mould.

Fain would I take with me all that is here. But how shall I?

A voice cannot carry the tongue and the lips that gave it wings. Alone must it seek the ether.

And alone and without his nest shall the eagle fly across the sun.

ولا هو خاطرة أتركها ورائي، بل فؤاداً زاده العطش
رقة والجوع حلاء.

رغم هذا لا أستطيع البقاء.
البحر الذي ينادي كل شيء لعبابه يناديني، وعلي أن
ألبي النداء.
فالبقاء، رغم اشتعال الساعات في الليل، تبلد وتبلر
وانكفاء.
ليتني أحمل كل ما هنا معي. لكن كيف لي؟
لا يستطيع الصوت حمل اللسان ولا الشفاه التي
وهبته الجناح. وحده عليه أن يشق الأثير،
ووحده بلا عشه قدر النسر عبر الشمس أن يطير.

Now when he reached the foot of the hill, he turned again towards the sea, and he saw his ship approaching the harbour, and upon her prow the mariners, the men of his own land.

And his soul cried out to them, and he said:

Sons of my ancient mother, you riders of the tides,

How often have you sailed in my dreams. And now you come in my awakening, which is my deeper dream.

Ready am I to go, and my eagerness with sails full set awaits the wind.

Only another breath will I breathe in this still air, only another loving look cast backward,

وإذ بلغ سفح التل استدار ثانية نحو البحر، فرأى السفينة تدنو من المرفأ، وعلى مقدمها البحارة، رجال من بلاده.

هفت روحه إليهم، فقال:
يا بني أمي والأزل، يا من تركبون الغمار،
لكم عبر شراعكم أحلامي. والآن في صحوتي تأتون، وصحوتي هي حلمي الأعمق.
إني جاهز للرحيل، وشوقي مشرع ينتظر الريح.
مرة واحدة سأعب من هذا الهواء الساكن، ونظرة حب واحدة سألقي ورائي،

And then I shall stand among you, a
seafarer among seafarers.

And you, vast sea, sleepless mother,

Who alone are peace and freedom to the
river and the stream,

Only another winding will this stream
make, only another murmur in this glade,

And then I shall come to you, a boundless
drop to a boundless ocean.

And as he walked he saw from afar men
and women leaving their fields and their
vineyards and hastening towards the city
gates.

And he heard their voices calling his
name, and shouting from field to field
telling one another of the coming of his
ship.

ثم أقف بينكم، بحاراً بين مبحرين.

وأنت، أيها البحر الكبير، أيا أماً لا تنام،

يا من وحده الحرية للنهر والسلام للغدير،

أمام هذا الجدول منعطف أخير، وله في الغيضة
خرير.

بعدها آتيك، قطرة لا حد لها في محيط بلا حدود.

وإذ مشى، رأى في البعد رجالاً ونساء يغادرون
حقولهم وكرومهم ويحثون الخطى إلى أبواب المدينة.

وسمع أصواتهم تلهج باسمه، ومن حقل لحقل
تتنادى، كلٌ يعلم الآخر بقدوم السفينة.

And he said to himself:

Shall the day of parting be the day of gathering?

And shall it be said that my eve was in truth my dawn?

And what shall I give unto him who has left his plough in midfurrow, or to him who has stopped the wheel of his winepress?

Shall my heart become a tree heavy-laden with fruit that I may gather and give unto them?

And shall my desires flow like a fountain that I may fill their cups?

Am I a harp that the hand of the mighty may touch me, or a flute that his breath may pass through me?

وقال لنفسه:

هل يكون يوم الفراق ذاته يوم اللقاء؟

هل يقال إن عشيتي كانت في الحقيقة فجري؟

وماذا أقدم لمن عاف محراثه في الثلم، أو أوقف معصرته عن الدوران؟

هل يصبح قلبي شجرة مثقلة بالثمر أقطفه لهم؟

هل تتدفق أشواقي نبعاً أملأ منه أقداحهم؟

أقيثارة أنا تلمسها يد القدير، أم ناي تعبره أنفاسه؟

A seeker of silences am I, and what treasure have I found in silences that I may dispense with confidence?

If this is my day of harvest, in what fields have I sowed the seeds, and in what unremembered seasons?

If this indeed be the hour in which I lift up my lantern, it is not my flame that shall burn therein.

Empty and dark shall I raise my lantern,

And the guardian of the night shall fill it with oil and he shall light it also.

These things he said in words. But much in his heart remained unsaid. For he himself could not speak his deeper secret.

ما أنا إلا طالب صمت، فأي كنز وجدت في
الصمت أفرقه بإيمان؟

إذا كان هذا يوم حصادي، فبأي حقول وأي فصول
منسية زرعت البذور؟

وإذا كانت هذه حقاً هي الساعة أرفع فيها مصباحي،
فليس لهيبي ما سيتوهج فيه.

مصباحي أرفعه خاوياً غير مضاء،
والعين التي تحرس الليل ستملؤه بالزيت وبالضياء.

قال هذا في كلمات. وبقي الكثير في قلبه بلا كلام.
فلم يكن ذاته قادراً على كشف سره الأعمق.

And when he entered into the city all the people came to meet him, and they were crying out to him as with one voice.

And the elders of the city stood forth and said:

Go not yet away from us.

A noontide have you been in our twilight, and your youth has given us dreams to dream.

No stranger are you among us, nor a guest, but our son and our dearly beloved.

Suffer not yet our eyes to hunger for your face.

وإذ دخل المدينة هب لرؤيته الناس جميعاً، ينادونه
كأنما بصوت واحد.

وتقدم الشيوخ وقالوا:

لا ترحل بعد عنا.

في غسق أيامنا كنت لنا ضحى، وشبابك أعطانا،
كي نحلم، الأحلام.

ما أنت بغريب بيننا، ولا بضيف، بل ابن وحبيب
غال.

فلا تدع عيوننا تكابد لمحياك.

And the priests and the priestesses said unto him:

Let not the waves of the sea separate us now, and the years you have spent in our midst become a memory.

You have walked among us a spirit, and your shadow has been a light upon our faces.

Much have we loved you. But speechless was our love, and with veils has it been veiled.

Yet now it cries aloud unto you, and would stand revealed before you.

And ever has it been that love knows not its own depth until the hour of separation.

وقال له الكهنة والكاهنات:

لا تدع أمواج البحر تفرقنا، ولا سنيك بيننا تصبح ذكرى.

روحاً سِرت بيننا، وظلك انداح على وجوهنا نوراً.

لكم أحببناك. كان حبنا أخرس. حجاب يخفيه وراء حجاب.

لكنه بلهفة يناديك الآن، ولسوف يقف أمامك في بَواح.

لم يعرف الحب يوماً عمقه حتى تَعجَل حمة الفِراق.

And others came also and entreated him. But he answered them not. He only bent his head; and those who stood near saw his tears falling upon his breast.

And he and the people proceeded towards the great square before the temple.

And there came out of the sanctuary a woman whose name was Almitra. And she was a seeress.

And he looked upon her with exceeding tenderness, for it was she who had first sought and believed in him when he had been but a day in their city.

And she hailed him, saying:

Prophet of God, in quest of the uttermost, long have you searched the distances for your ship.

وجاء آخرون أيضاً ضارعين. فلم ينبس. أطرق؛
ورأى الواقفون بقربه على صدره تسّاقطُ العبرات.
ثم تقدم والناس إلى الميدان الكبير قبالة المعبد.

ومن الحرم المقدس خرجت امرأة اسمها ألمِطرا، عرافة
تستبصر الأيام.
بفائض الحنان رنا إليها، كانت أول من سعى إليه
وآمن به ولمّا يكن مضى عليه في المدينة غير ساعات.
حيته، قائلة:
يا ملهماً ألهمه الله، يا باحثاً عن أسمى الغايات،
بحثك عن شراعك في الآفاق طال.

And now your ship has come, and you must needs go.

Deep is your longing for the land of your memories and the dwelling place of your greater desires; and our love would not bind you nor our needs hold you.

Yet this we ask ere you leave us, that you speak to us and give us of your truth.

And we will give it unto our children, and they unto their children, and it shall not perish.

In your aloneness you have watched with our days, and in your wakefulness you have listened to the weeping and laughter of our sleep.

Now therefore disclose us to ourselves, and tell us all that has been shown you of that which is between birth and death.

وسفينتك الآن جاءت، وآن أن تشد الرحال.

عميق شوقك لمهد ذكرياتك وعظيم أمانيك؛ وحبنا لن يقيدك، وحاجاتنا لن تبقيك.

لكن قبل أن تغادرنا، نطلب أن تحدثنا ومن واقع أمرك تعطينا ما أوتيت.

فنعطيه لأبنائنا، فيعطوه لأبنائهم، فلا يضيع.

في انفرادك راقبت مع أيامنا، وفي صحوك أصغيت لضحكنا ونحيبنا في نومنا.

فأطلعنا على سرنا، وأخبرنا بما بصُرت به من الذي بين الولادة والموت.

And he answered:

People of Orphalese, of what can I speak save of that which is even now moving within your souls?

فأجاب:

يا معشر أورفليس، عمّ أتكلم ولا يمور في أرواحكم الآن وكل آن؟

THEN said Almitra, Speak to us of **Love**.

And he raised his head and looked upon the people, and there fell a silence upon them. And with a great voice he said:

When love beckons to you, follow him,

Though his ways are hard and steep.

And when his wings enfold you yield to him,

Though the sword hidden among his pinions may wound you.

And when he speaks to you believe in him,

Though his voice may shatter your dreams as the north wind lays waste the garden.

قالت ألمطرا، حدثنا عن الحب.

فرفع رأسه ونظر إلى الناس، فحل عليهم صمت.

فقال بصوت عظيم:

إذا أومأ الحب لكم اتبعوه،

ولو كانت دروبه صعبة وفي انحدار.

وإذا ضمكم بجناحه أطيعوه،

ولو أدماكم في ريشه السيف الخفي.

وإذا حدثكم صدقوه،

ولو عصف صوته بأحلامكم عصف الشّمأل

بالرَوض.

For even as love crowns you so shall he crucify you. Even as he is for your growth so is he for your pruning.

Even as he ascends to your heights and caresses your tenderest branches that quiver in the sun,

So shall he descend to your roots and shake them in their clinging to the earth.

Like sheaves of corn he gathers you unto himself.

He threshes you to make you naked.

He sifts you to free you from your husks.

He grinds you to whiteness.

He kneads you until you are pliant;

And then he assigns you to his sacred fire that you may become sacred bread for God's sacred feast.

مثلما يتوجكم الحب، يوثقكم بصليب الآلام. مثلما
ينمي عودكم، يشذب العود في آن.
مثلما يصعد إلى عليائكم ويداعب أرق أغصانكم
المرتعشة في الشمس،
سيهبط إلى جذوركم ويهز لحمتها بالتراب.
يضمكم إليه حزم سنابل.
يدرسكم ليعريَكم.
ينخلكم ليحرركم من قشوركم.
يطحنكم إلى بياض.
يحيلكم عجيناً طوياً؛
ثم يوْكِلكم قدس ناره لتصيروا خبز قدسٍ لقداس الله.

All these things shall love do unto you
that you may know the secrets of your
heart, and in that knowledge become a
fragment of Life's heart.

But if in your fear you would seek only
love's peace and love's pleasure,
    Then it is better for you that you cover
your nakedness and pass out of love's
threshing-floor,
    Into the seasonless world where you shall
laugh, but not all of your laughter, and
weep, but not all of your tears.

Love gives naught but itself and takes
naught but from itself.
    Love possesses not nor would it be
possessed;

كل هذا يفعله الحب بكم لتعرفوا أسرار قلوبكم،

ولتضحوا بالمعرفة فلذة في كبد الحياة.

لكن إنْ في خوفكم لم تنشدوا إلا وئام الحب ومتعة الحب،

فأولى أن تستروا عريَكم وترحلوا عن بيدر الحب،

إلى العالم الذي لا فصول فيه، حيث تضحكون،

ولكن ليس كل ضحككم، وتذرفون، ولكن ليس كل ما في مآقيكم من دموع.

لا يعطي الحب إلا ذاته ولا يأخذ إلا من ذاته.

لا يملِك الحب ولا يقبل بأن يُملَك.

For love is sufficient unto love.

When you love you should not say, 'God is in my heart,' but rather, 'I am in the heart of God.'
And think not that you can direct the course of love, for love, if it finds you worthy, directs your course.

Love has no other desire but to fulfil itself.
But if you love and must needs have desires, let these be your desires:
To melt and be like a running brook that sings its melody to the night;
To know the pain of too much tenderness.

فالحب يكفيه الحب.

عندما تحب، لا تقل 'إن الله في قلبي،' بل 'إني في قلب الله.'

ولا يراودك أنك قادر على توجيه خطى الحب، فالحب، إن وجدك أهلاً، يرسم لك الاتجاه.

لا رغبة للحب إلا تحقيق ذاته.

فإن أحببت وكانت لك رغائب، فلتكن رغائبك هذه:

أن تذوب وتجري كالغدير ينشد لليل لحنه.

أن تعرف ألم الحنان عندما الحنان يرسل دفقه.

To be wounded by your own understanding of love;

And to bleed willingly and joyfully.

To wake at dawn with a winged heart and give thanks for another day of loving;

To rest at the noon hour and meditate love's ecstasy;

To return home at eventide with gratitude;

And then to sleep with a prayer for the beloved in your heart and a song of praise upon your lips.

أن يدميك فهمك للحب؛

وتنزف بفرح وطيب خاطر.

أن تستيقظ في الفجر بقلب ذي جناح وتحمد الله على

يوم حب؛

أن تستريح في الظهيرة وتتأمل نشوة الحب؛

أن تعود إلى بيتك في المساء بعرفان؛

فتنام وفي قلبك للحبيب صلاة وعلى شفتيك أغنية

مديح له.

THEN Almitra spoke again and said, And what of **Marriage**, Master?

And he answered, saying:

You were born together, and together you shall be forevermore.

You shall be together when the white wings of death scatter your days.

Aye, you shall be together even in the silent memory of God.

But let there be spaces in your togetherness.

And let the winds of the heavens dance between you.

Love one another, but make not a bond of love:

Let it rather be a moving sea between the shores of your souls.

وتكلمت ألمطرا ثانية، وقالت، وماذا عن **الزواج**،
يا سيدي؟

فأجاب:

ولدتما معاً، ومعاً تبقيان أبد السنين.

ستكونان معاً حين تبعثر أجنحة الموت البيضاء
أيامكما.

أجل، وستكونان معاً في ذاكرة الله الصامتة.

فاجعلا في جمعكما فسحاً،

ولترقص بينكما رياح النعيم.

تبادلا الحب، ولا تجعلا منه وثاقاً،

بل بحراً يتماوج بين روحك وروحه.

Fill each other's cup but drink not from one cup.

Give one another of your bread but eat not from the same loaf.

Sing and dance together and be joyous, but let each one of you be alone,

Even as the strings of a lute are alone though they quiver with the same music.

Give your hearts, but not into each other's keeping.

For only the hand of Life can contain your hearts.

And stand together yet not too near together:

For the pillars of the temple stand apart,

And the oak tree and the cypress grow not in each other's shadow.

املئي كأسه وليملأ كأسك ولا تشربا من كأس واحد.

قدمي من خبزك له وليقدم لك من خبزه ولا تأكلا من رغيف واحد.

غنيا وارقصا معاً وافرحا، وليدع كلٌّ الآخر وحده، كأوتار العود وحدها رغم ارتعاشها مع اللحن الواحد.

ليهب كلٌّ قلبه، ولا تتركاه في جَعبة الآخر يبقى.

وحدها يد الحياة قادرة على احتواء قلبك وقلبه.

وقفا معاً لكن دون التصاق:

فأعمدة المعبد تباعد بعضها عن بعض،

وشجرة السرو وشجرة السنديان لا تنموان كلٌّ في ظل الأخرى.

AND a woman who held a babe against her bosom said, Speak to us of **Children**.

And he said:

Your children are not your children.

They are the sons and daughters of Life's longing for itself.

They come through you but not from you,

And though they are with you yet they belong not to you.

You may give them your love but not your thoughts,

For they have their own thoughts.

You may house their bodies but not their souls,

ثم قالت امرأة تضم رضيعاً، حدثنا عن **الأبناء**.

فقال:

أبناؤكم ليسوا أبناءكم.

هم أولاد وبنات الحياة إذ لذاتها تتوق الحياة.

يأتون من خلالكم وليس منكم،

ورغم أنهم معكم فإنهم لا ينتمون إليكم.

قد تمنحونهم حبكم لا أفكاركم،

أفكارهم خاصة بهم.

قد تؤوون أجسادهم لا أرواحهم،

Their souls dwell in the house of
tomorrow, which you cannot visit, not
even in your dreams.

You may strive to be like them, but seek
not to make them like you.

For life goes not backward nor tarries
with yesterday.

You are the bows from which your
children as living arrows are sent forth.

The Archer sees the mark upon the path
of the infinite, and He bends you with His
might that His arrows may go swift and far.

Let your bending in the Archer's hand be
for gladness;

For even as he loves the arrow that flies,
so He loves also the bow that is stable.

أرواحهم تسكن منازل الغد التي لا سبيل لكم إليها،
حتى في أحلامكم.
قد تجهدون لتكونوا مثلهم، لكن لا تحاولوا أن
تجعلوهم مثلكم.
فالحياة لا تمضي في رجوع ولا تتلبث في الأمس
الفائت.
أنتم الأقواس سهاماً حية يطلَق منها أبناؤكم.

يرى الرامي على درب المطلق العلامة، فيلويكم
جبروته لتحلق سهامه خاطفة إلى البعيد.
فليكن لَيّكم بيد الرامي ابتهاجاً؛
فإنه يحب السهم المحلق، كما يحب القوس الثابت.

THEN said a rich man, Speak to us of **Giving**.

And he answered:

You give but little when you give of your possessions.

It is when you give of yourself that you truly give.

For what are your possessions but things you keep and guard for fear you may need them tomorrow?

And tomorrow, what shall tomorrow bring to the over-prudent dog burying bones in the trackless sand as he follows the pilgrims to the holy city?

And what is fear of need but need itself?

Is not dread of thirst when your well is full the thirst that is unquenchable?

ثم قال رجل ثري، حدثنا عن **العطاء**،
فأجاب:
عطاؤكم مما ملكت أيديكم قليل.
عطاؤكم من ذاتكم هو العطاء الصادق.
وهل ممتلكاتكم إلا أشياء تحفظونها وتحرسونها خشية
إملاق في غد قادم؟
والغد، ماذا يجلب الغد لجرو زائد الحرص، يدفن
العظام، تحسباً، برمل لا يحفظ أثراً بينما يتبع إلى
المدينة المقدسة الحجيج؟
وهل الفزع من العوز إلا العوز ذاته؟
أليس الخوف من العطش وبئرك طافحة، عطشاً لا
سبيل إلى إروائه؟

There are those who give little of the much which they have, and they give it for recognition and their hidden desire makes their gifts unwholesome.

And there are those who have little and give it all.

These are the believers in life and the bounty of life, and their coffer is never empty.

There are those who give with joy, and that joy is their reward.

And there are those who give with pain, and that pain is their baptism.

And there are those who give and know not pain in giving, nor do they seek joy, nor give with mindfulness of virtue;

They give as in yonder valley the myrtle breathes its fragrance into space.

هناك من يعطي القليل من الكثير مما لديه طمعاً
بصيت فيحيل ما في سريرته عطاياه فساداً.
وهناك من يملك القليل ويهبه جميعاً.
هم المؤمنون بالحياة وبجودها، لا ينضب معينهم
أبداً.

وهناك من يعطي بغبطة، وغبطتهم هي جزاؤهم.
وهناك من يعطي بألم وألمهم تطهير لهم.
وهناك من يعطي ولا يعرف في عطائه ألماً ولا يبتغي
فرحاً ولا احتساباً لشيمة أو فضيلة؛
يعطي كما في ذينك الوادي يتضوع الآس بالعبير.

Through the hand of such as these God speaks, and from behind their eyes He smiles upon the earth.

It is well to give when asked, but it is better to give unasked, through understanding;
And to the open-handed the search for one who shall receive is joy greater than giving.
And is there aught you would withhold?
All you have shall some day be given;
Therefore give now, that the season of giving may be yours and not your inheritors'.

You often say, 'I would give, but only to the deserving.'

عبر أيدي هؤلاء يتكلم الله، ومن خلف عيونهم يحنو
على الأديم.

حسن عطاؤكم بطلب، والأفضل بلا طلب، عبر
الفهم؛
فالبحث عن متلق لباسط اليد فرح يفوق العطاء ذاته.
وهل هناك ما تبقيه؟
كلُ ما لَكَ مآلُكَ أن تعطيه؛
فأعطه الآن يكن موسم العطاء موسمك لا موسم
وريثك.

غالباً ما تقول، 'سأعطي، ولكن لمن يستحق.'

The trees in your orchard say not so, nor the flock in your pasture.

They give that they may live, for to withhold is to perish.

Surely he who is worthy to receive his days and his nights is worthy of all else from you.

And he who has deserved to drink from the ocean of life deserves to fill his cup from your little stream.

And what desert greater shall there be, than that which lies in the courage and the confidence, nay the charity, of receiving?

And who are you that men should rend their bosom and unveil their pride, that you may see their worth naked and their pride unabashed?

هذا لا تقوله الأشجار في بستانك، ولا القطعان في مراعيك.

هذه تعطي لتحيا، فالإمساك عن العطاء موت.

من استحق أن يوهَب أيامه ولياليه، جدير بكل شيء آخر منك.

ومن استحق أن يسقى من بحر الحياة، يستأهل ملء كأسه من غديرك الصغير.

وأي مثوبة هناك أعظم من التي في شجاعة وإيمان، بل إحسان التلقي؟

ومن تكون حتى يشق الرجال لك عن صدورهم ويعرّوا كبرياءهم، لترى استحقاقهم بلا ستر وكبرياءهم بلا حياء؟

See first that you yourself deserve to be a giver, and an instrument of giving.

For in truth it is life that gives unto life – while you, who deem yourself a giver, are but a witness.

And you receivers – and you are all receivers – assume no weight of gratitude, lest you lay a yoke upon yourself and upon him who gives.

Rather rise together with the giver on his gifts as on wings;

For to be over-mindful of your debt is to doubt his generosity who had the free-hearted earth for mother, and God for father.

تأكد أولاً أنك، ذاتك، جدير بأن تكون مانحاً وأداة عطاء.

إنما الحياة تعطي للحياة وما أنت، يا من تظن نفسك مانحاً، إلا شاهد عطاء.

ويا أيها المتلقون- وكلكم متلق- لا تحملوا منّة لأحد تثقلون بنيرها كاهلكم وكاهل من أزجى العطاء.

أحرى أن تصعدوا مع من أعطى فوق عطاياه كمن على جناح؛

فالإسراف في التفكر بديونكم شك بكرم مَن اتخذ الأرض السخية أمّاً، والله أباً.

THEN an old man, a keeper of an inn, said, Speak to us of **Eating and Drinking**.

And he said:

Would that you could live on the fragrance of the earth, and like an air plant be sustained by the light.

But since you must kill to eat, and rob the newly born of its mother's milk to quench your thirst, let it then be an act of worship,

And let your board stand an altar on which the pure and the innocent of forest and plain are sacrificed for that which is purer and still more innocent in man.

When you kill a beast say to him in your heart:

'By the same power that slays you, I too am slain; and I too shall be consumed.

ثم قال كهل يدير نزلاً، حدثنا عن **الطعام والشراب**.

فقال:

ليتكم تعيشون على عبير الأرض، وكنبت الهواء تقتاتون بالضياء.

أمّا وقد أحل لكم القتل للأكل، ومن أمه سلب حليب الرضيع رياً لعطشكم، فليكن ذلك فعل عبادة.

لتكن مائدتكَ مذبحاً للنقي والبريء في السهل والغابة، فداء لما هو أكثر نقاء وأكثر براءة في الإنسان.

عندما تقتل بهيمة، قل في قلبك لها:

'إن القدرة التي تذبحك ستفتك بي أيضاً؛ فأنا كذلك سأفنى،

For the law that delivered you into my hand shall deliver me into a mightier hand.

Your blood and my blood is naught but the sap that feeds the tree of heaven.'

And when you crush an apple with your teeth, say to it in your heart:

'Your seeds shall live in my body,

And the buds of tomorrow shall blossom in my heart,

And your fragrance shall be my breath,

And together we shall rejoice through all the seasons.'

فالقانون الذي أسلمك ليدي سيسلمني ليد أكثر بطشاً،
فما دمي ودمك إلا النسغ الذي يروي أوراق الجنة.'

وعندما تقضم تفاحة، قل في قلبك لها:
'بذورك ستحيا في جسدي،
وسيزهر غدك في قلبي،
عبيرك سيصبح أنفاسي،
ومعاً سنفرح عبر الفصول.'

And in the autumn, when you gather the grapes of your vineyards for the winepress, say in your heart:

'I too am a vineyard, and my fruit shall be gathered for the winepress,

And like new wine I shall be kept in eternal vessels.'

And in winter, when you draw the wine, let there be in your heart a song for each cup;

And let there be in the song a remembrance for the autumn days, and for the vineyard, and for the winepress.

وفي الخريف، وأنت تجمع الكرمة للعصر، قل في
قلبك:

'إني أيضاً بستان وثماري ستقطف للعصر،
وكخمرة عصرت تواً ستحفظني خوابٍ للدهر.'
وفي الشتاء، وأنت ترشف النبيذ، اجعل لكل كأس في
قلبك أغنية؛

تحمل رجع أيام الخريف، والمعصرة، والكرم.

.

THEN a ploughman said, Speak to us of **Work**.

And he answered, saying:

You work that you may keep pace with the earth and the soul of the earth.

For to be idle is to become a stranger unto the seasons, and to step out of life's procession that marches in majesty and proud submission towards the infinite.

When you work you are a flute through whose heart the whispering of the hours turns to music.

Which of you would be a reed, dumb and silent, when all else sings together in unison?

ثم قال فلاح، حدثنا عن **العمل**،
فأجاب، قائلاً:
تعملون لتواكبوا خطى الأرض وروح الأرض،
فالتقاعس غربة عن الفصول، وخروج عن موكب
الحياة السائر نحو المطلق بجلال وطاعة كبرياء.

عندما تعمل تغدو ناياً عبر حشاشته يتحول همس
الساعات إلى أنغام.
من يقبل أن يكون قصبة صماء بكماء وكل ما حوله
يغني في انسجام؟

Always you have been told that work is a curse and labour a misfortune.

But I say to you that when you work you fulfil a part of earth's furthest dream, assigned to you when the dream was born,

And in keeping yourself with labour you are in truth loving life,

And to love life through labour is to be intimate with life's inmost secret.

But if you in your pain call birth an affliction and the support of the flesh a curse written upon your brow, then I answer that naught but the sweat of your brow shall wash away that which is written.

دائماً ما قيل لكم إن العمل لعنة والكد بلاء.

وأقول لكم، إنكم تحققون بالعمل جزءاً من أبعد أحلام الأرض، أوكل لكم حينما ولد الحلم،

وقيل لكم، إنكم بمواصلتكم العمل تواصلون حب الحياة،

وحب الحياة بالعمل ألفة مع أعمق أسرار الحياة.

لكن إنْ في آلامكم قلتم إنَ الولادة بلوى، وإقامة الصُلب لعنة مكتوبة على جبينكم، فأجيب فأقول، لا يمحو المكتوب إلا عرق الجبين.

You have been told also that life is darkness, and in your weariness you echo what was said by the weary.

And I say that life is indeed darkness save when there is urge,

And all urge is blind save when there is knowledge,

And all knowledge is vain save when there is work,

And all work is empty save when there is love;

And when you work with love you bind yourself to yourself, and to one another, and to God.

And what is it to work with love?

وقيل لكم أيضاً، إن الحياة ظلمة، فرحتم في سأمكم ترددون ما قاله السؤوم.

وأقول، إن الحياة حقاً ظلمة إلا إذا كان هناك دافع،

وإن كل دافع أعمى إلا إذا كان هناك علم،

وإن كل علم باطل إلا إذا كان هناك عمل،

وإن كل عمل فارغ إلا إذا كان هناك حب؛

وعندما تعمل بحب توثق ذاتك مع ذاتك، ومع غيرك، وربك.

ما هو العمل بحب؟

It is to weave the cloth with threads drawn from your heart, even as if your beloved were to wear that cloth.

It is to build a house with affection, even as if your beloved were to dwell in that house.

It is to sow seeds with tenderness and reap the harvest with joy, as if your beloved were to eat the fruit.

It is to charge all things you fashion with a breath of your own spirit.

And to know that all the blessed dead are standing about you and watching.

Often have I heard you say, as if speaking in sleep, 'He who works in marble, and finds the shape of his own soul in the stone, is nobler than he who ploughs the soil.

هو أن تحوك الثوب بخيوط من جَنانك، كأن الثوب
رداء الحبيب.
هو أن تشيد بيتاً بإحساس، كأن البيت مقام الحبيب.
هو أن تنثر البذور بحنان وتحصد الغلال بابتهاج،
كأن الثمار طعام الحبيب.
وأن تبث ما تصوغه يداك بنفح من خالص ذاتك،
وتعلم أن الذين بوركوا بالموت واقفون يراقبون حولك.

لكم سمعتكم تقولون، كمن في المنام يقول، 'إن
العامل في الرخام يرى في الحجر شكل روحه، لأنبل
ممن يفلح الأرض بمحراث.

67

And he who seizes the rainbow to lay it on a cloth in the likeness of man, is more than he who makes the sandals for your feet.'

But I say, not in sleep, but in the over-wakefulness of noontide, that the wind speaks no more sweetly to the giant oaks than to the least of all the blades of grass;

And he alone is great who turns the voice of the wind into a song made sweater by his own loving.

Work is love made visible.

And if you cannot work with love but only with distaste, it is better that you should leave your work and sit at the gate of the temple and take alms of those who work with joy.

وإن القابض على قوس قزح يطبعه في رداء على صورة إنسان، لأفضل ممن يصنع للقدمين الحذاء.'

لكني أقول، في ذروة اليقظة، لا في المنام، إن الريح تبث حلو الكلام أصغر الحشائش كما تبث عالي السنديان؛

وإن العظيم هو وحده الذي يحيل صوت الريح أغنية زادت بحب قلبه الحنان.

العمل حب تجلى.

فإن لم تستطع العمل بحب، بل بتأفف، فأولى أن تهجر العمل وتقعد على باب المعبد تمد يداً للصدقات ممن يعملون بابتهاج.

For if you bake bread with indifference, you bake a bitter bread that feeds but half man's hunger.

And if you grudge the crushing of the grapes, your grudge distils a poison in the wine.

And if you sing though as angels, and love not the singing, you muffle man's ears to the voices of the day and the voices of the night.

فإن أنت أنضجت خبزك بلا اهتمام، خرج الخبز مر
المذاق لا يسد رمق إنسان.

وإن كرهت سحق العنب، تقطر كرهك سماً في النبيذ.

وإن غنيت، حتى غناء ملائكة، ولم تحب النشيد،
لصممت آذان الإنسان عن أصوات النهار وأصوات
الليل.

THEN a woman said, Speak to us of **Joy and Sorrow**.

And he answered:

Your joy is your sorrow unmasked.

And the selfsame well from which your laughter rises was oftentimes filled with your tears.

And how else can it be?

The deeper that sorrow carves into your being, the more joy you can contain.

Is not the cup that holds your wine the very cup that was burned in the potter's oven?

And is not the loot that soothes your spirit the very wood that was hollowed with knives?

ثم قالت امرأة، حدثنا عن **الفرح والحزن**،
فأجاب:

فرحكِ هو حزنكِ بلا قناع.

والبئر التي تطفح بضحكك هي عينها التي فاضت
بدمعك.

وكيف يكون الأمر غير ذلك؟

كلما زاد الحزن حفراً في كيانك، كبر الفرح الذي
يحتويه الكيان.

أليس الكوب الذي يضم نبيذك عينه الذي احترق في
أتون الخزاف؟

أليس العود الذي للحنه روحك تستكين عينه الذي
حفرته السكين؟

73

When you are joyous, look deep into your heart and you shall find it is only that which has given you sorrow is giving you joy.

When you are sorrowful, look again in your heart and you shall see that in truth you are weeping for that which has been your delight.

Some of you say, 'Joy is greater than sorrow,' and others say, Nay, sorrow is the greater.'

But I say unto you, they are inseparable.

Together they come, and when one sits alone with you at your board, remember that the other is asleep upon your bed.

في فرحك، انظري ملياً في قلبك، ولسوف ترين أن ما أعطاك حزنك هو ما يعطيك فرحك.

وفي حزنكِ، انظري ثانية في قلبك، ولسوف ترين أن ما أرسل دمعك هو الذي كان ولايزال بهجتك.

بعضكم يقول، 'إن الفرح أعظم من الحزن،' ويقول آخرون، 'كلا، إن الحزن أعظم.'

لكني أقول، إنهما لا ينفصلان.

معاً يأتيان، فإذا جلس أحدهما على طعامك، تذكري أن الآخر غاف على سريرك.

Verily you are suspended like scales
between your sorrow and your joy.

Only when you are empty are you at
standstill and balanced.
When the treasure-keeper lifts you to
weigh his gold and his silver, needs must
your joy or your sorrow rise or fall.

كالميزان أنت لا ريب معلقة بين حزنك وفرحك.

لا يستقيم قائمك ولا يستوي ميزانك إلا في فراغك.

وعندما يرفعك الخازن ليزن ذهبه وفضته، فلا بد أن

يهبط فرحك أو يشيل، أو يهبط أو يشيل حزنك.

THEN a mason came forth and said, Speak to us of **Houses**.

And he answered and said:

Build of your imaginings a bower in the wilderness ere you build a house within the city walls.

For even as you have home-comings in your twilight, so has the wanderer in you, the ever-distant and alone.

Your house is your larger body.

It grows in the sun and sleeps in the stillness of the night; and it is not dreamless. Does not your house dream? And dreaming, leave the city for grove or hilltop?

Would that I could gather your houses into my hand, and like a sower scatter them in forest and meadow.

ثم تقدم بنّاء وقال، حدثنا عن **البيوت**، فأجاب:

أقيموا من الخيال عريشة في البراري قبل أن تشيدوا في المدينة بيتاً بسور.

تعود إلى بيتك في العشي، وكذلك الهائم فيك يعود، ذلك البعيد أبداً، ذلك الوحيد.

بيتك هو جسدك الأكبر.

في الشمس ينمو، وفي سكون الليل ينام؛ ولا يعدَم الأحلام. أولا يحلم بيتك؟ وفي حلمه، ألا يغادر المدينة إلى تل أو أيك؟

ليتني أجمع بيوتكم في راحتي، وكالزارع أنثرها في المرج والغابة.

Would the valleys were your streets, and the green paths your alleys, that you might seek one another through vineyards, and come with the fragrance of the earth in your garments.

But these things are not yet to be.
In their fear your forefathers gathered you too near together. And that fear shall endure a little longer. A little longer shall your city walls separate your hearths from your fields.

And tell me, people of Orphalese, what have you in these houses? And what is it you guard with fastened doors?

Have you peace, the quiet urge that reveals your power?

ليتها الوديان كانت دروبكم، والممرات الخضر
سبلكم، فيسعى بعضكم إلى بعض عبر الكروم،
فتتلاقون وعبير الأرض في ثيابكم.
لكن هيهاتِ ذلك أن يكون.
في خوفهم قرب أجدادكم ما بينكم. ولسوف يبقى
الخوف حيناً. وحيناً ستفصل جدران مدينتكم حقولكم عن
جانب-ناركم.

يا أهل أورفليس، سألتكم، ماذا في هذي البيوت
تخبئون؟ وبأبواب موصدة تحرسون؟
هل لديكم سلام، الدافع الهادئ الذي يشحذ هممكم؟

Have you remembrances, the glimmering arches that span the summits of the mind?

Have you beauty, that leads the heart from things fashioned of wood and stone to the holy mountain?

Tell me, have you these in your houses?

Or have you only comfort, and the lust for comfort, that stealthy thing that enters the house a guest, and then becomes a host, and then a master?

Ay, and it becomes a tamer, and with hook and scourge makes puppets of your larger desires.

Though its hands are silken, its heart is of iron.

It lulls you to sleep only to stand by your bed and jeer at the dignity of the flesh.

هل لديكم ذكريات، القناطر المشعة بين ذرى العقل بالنور؟

هل لديكم جمال، هذا الذي يقود القلب من زخرف الخشب ودمى الحجارة إلى الجبل الطهور؟

أخبروني، هل تملكون هذه في بيوتكم؟

أم أن ما تملكونه راحة، وشهوة راحة، متسلل يدخل البيت ضيفاً، فيصبح مضيفاً، ثم سيداً؟

أجل، ويصبح مروضاً، بحبل وكُلّاب يحيل أمانيكم العظام دمى.

يداه من حرير، لكن قلبه من حديد.

يهدهدكم حتى تناموا، فيقف على سريركم ساخراً بوقار عريكم.

It makes mock of your sound senses, and lays them in thistledown like fragile vessels.

Verily the lust for comfort murders the passion of the soul, and walks grinning in the funeral.

But you children of space, you restless in rest, you shall not be trapped or tamed.

Your house shall not be an anchor but a mast.

It shall not be a glistening film that covers a wound, but an eyelid that guards the eye.

You shall not fold your wings that you may pass through doors, nor bend your heads that they strike not against a ceiling, nor fear to breathe lest walls should crack and fall down.

ويهزأ بأحاسيسكم السليمة، ويودعها زغب الريش كآنية قصِمة وبلّور رقيق.

نعم، شهوة الراحة تقتل شغف الروح، وتسير هازئة في جنازة القتيل.

لكنكم، يا أبناء الأثير، يا من في الراحة تضيقون، لن تقعوا في الشرَك ولن يروضكم حرير.

لن يكون بيتك مرساة، بل شراعاً.

هو جَفن يحرس العين، ولن يكون لجرح ضماداً.

لن تطووا الجناح لتعبروا الأبواب، ولن تطأطئوا كيلا ترتطم رؤوسكم بسقف، ولن تتهيبوا التنفس خشية أن تتصدع وتهبط جدر في البيت.

You shall not dwell in tombs made by the dead for the living.

And though of magnificence and splendour, your house shall not hold your secret nor shelter your longing.

For that which is boundless in you abides in the mansion of the sky, whose door is the morning mist, and whose windows are the songs and the silences of night.

لن تسكنوا أضرحة بناها ميت لحي.

ورغم الأبهة والبهاء، لن يتسع بيتك لسرك ولن يكون ملاذاً لشوقك.

فالواسع اللانهائي فيك يسكن رحاب سماء، ضباب الصبح الرقيق بابها، وشبابيكها سكنات الليل وتراتيل المساء.

AND the weaver said, Speak to us of **Clothes**.

And he answered:

Your clothes conceal much of your beauty, yet they hide not the unbeautiful.

And though you seek in garments the freedom of privacy you may find in them a harness and a chain.

Would that you could meet the sun and the wind with more of your skin and less of your raiment.

For the breath of life is in the sunlight and the hand of life is in the wind.

Some of you say, 'It is the north wind who has woven the clothes we wear.'

And I say, Ay, it was the north wind,

وقال الحائك، حدثنا عن **الثياب**،

فأجاب:

ملابسكم تحجب جل جمالكم، ولا تخفي ما هو غير جميل.

تنشدون حرية الاختلاء في اللباس وربما وجدتموه لجاماً وقيداً.

ليتكم تخرجون للشمس والريح بكثير بشرتكم وقليل لباسكم.

ففي نور الشمس أنفاس الحياة، وفي الريح يدها.

بعضكم يقول، 'ريح الشمَال نسجت ما نرتديه.'

وأقول، بلى، هي الشمأل،

But shame was his loom, and the softening of the sinews was his thread.

And when his work was done he laughed in the forest.

Forget not that modesty is for a shield against the eye of the unclean.

And when the unclean shall be no more, what were modesty but a fetter and a fouling of the mind?

And forget not that the earth delights to feel your bare feet and the winds long to play with your hair.

لكن الحياء كان نولها وارتخاء العصب الخيط.

فلما أتمت العمل قهقهت في عمق الغيط.

لا تنسوا أن غاية الاحتشام هي أن يكون درعاً يفقأ عين الفجر.

لكن، ماذا يمسي الاحتشام بعد زوال الفجر غير أسر وفساد فكر؟

ولا تنسوا أن الأرض تعشق لمس أقدامكم وهي عارية، وأن الريح تصبو لمداعبة الشعر.

AND a merchant said, Speak to us of
Buying and Selling.

And he answered and said:

To you the earth yields her fruit, and you
shall not want if you but know how to fill
your hands.

It is in exchanging the gifts of the earth
that you shall find abundance and be
satisfied.

Yet, unless the exchange be in love and
kindly justice, it will but lead some to greed
and others to hunger.

When in the market place you toilers of
the sea and fields and vineyards meet the
weavers and the potters and the gatherers of
spices,-

وقال تاجر، حدثنا عن البيع والشراء،
فأجاب:

تطرح الأرض الثمار لكم، ولن تملَقوا إن أحسنتم مَلء الكف.

في تبادل خيرات الأرض الفيض والكفاية والرضى.

فإن لم يجر التبادل بحب وعدل رحيم، فلسوف يكون هناك الطامع ولسوف يكون هناك الجائع.

يا من في البحر وفي الحقول والكروم تكدون، عندما في ساحة السوق تلقون النساج والخزاف وتاجر التوابل والبقول،ـ

Invoke then the master spirit of the earth, to come into your midst and sanctify the scales and the reckoning that weigh value against value.

And suffer not the barren-handed to take part in your transactions, who would sell their words for your labour.

To such men you should say,

'Come with us to the field, or go with our brothers to the sea and cast your net;

For the land and the sea shall be bountiful to you even as to us.'

And if there come the singers and the dancers and the flute players,- buy of their gifts also.

استحضروا روح الأرض الصمد فيحِل بينكم فيقضي الحسبة ويقيم الميزان الذي يزن الأثمان بالأثمان.

ولا تَدَعوا فارغ اليد يشارك في تجارتكم، فيبادل بالكلام كدكم.

له ولمثله قولوا،

'تعالوا معنا إلى الحقل، أو اذهبوا مع إخواننا إلى البحر ترمون فيه شباككم؛

فالبر والبحر وفر لنا، وسيكونان كذلك لكم.'

وإن جاء المنشد والراقص وعازف العود فاشرَوا من مواهبهم أيضاً.

For they too are gatherers of fruit and frankincense, and that which they bring, though fashioned of dreams, is raiment and food for your soul.

And before you leave the market place, see that no one has gone his way with empty hands.

For the master spirit of the earth shall not sleep peacefully upon the wind till the needs of the least of you are satisfied.

فهم كذلك جامعو ثمار وبخور، وما يأتون به، وإن من نسج الأحلام، كساء وغذاء للروح.

وقبل أن تغادروا السوق، تأكدوا أن أحداً لم يَؤب فارغ اليدين.
فروح الأرض الأكبر لن ينام قرير العين على جناح الريح حتى تلبَى حاجة الأصغرَين.

THEN one of the judges of the city stood forth and said, Speak to us of **Crime and Punishment**.

And he answered, saying:

It is when your spirit goes wandering upon the wind,

That you, alone and unguarded, commit a wrong unto others and therefore unto yourself.

And for that wrong committed must you knock and wait a while unheeded at the gate of the blessed.

Like the ocean is your god-self;
It remains forever undefiled.
And like the ether it lifts but the winged.
Even like the sun is your god-self;

ثم تقدم قاض من المدينة وقال، حدثنا عن **الجريمة والعقاب**،

فأجاب:

عندما على دروب الريح روحكم تهيم،

بلا رفيق ولا رقيب تأتون إثماً يصيب الخلق وبذات الإثم تصابون.

فإذا حتم عليكم جراء ما اقترفتم طرق باب الصالحين والانتظار بلا جواب لحين.

كالمحيط ذاتكم الإلهية؛

إلى الأبد تبقى بلا دنس،

وكالأثير ترفع ذا الجناح.

وهي كالشمس حتى؛

It knows not the ways of the mole nor seeks it the holes of the serpent.

But your god-self dwells not alone in your being.

Much in you is still man, and much in you is not yet man,

But a shapeless pigmy that walks asleep in the mist searching for its own awakening.

And of the man in you would I now speak.

For it is he and not your god-self nor the pigmy in the mist, that knows crime and the punishment of crime.

Oftentimes have I heard you speak of one who commits a wrong as though he were not one of you, but a stranger unto you and an intruder upon your world.

لا تعرف مسالك الخلد ولا تقصِد لجحور الثعبان.

لكن ذاتكم الإلهية لا تسكن وحدها كيانكم.

كثير فيكم ما زال إنساناً، وكثير ليس بعد بإنسان، بل قزَم بلا شكل يسير نائماً في الضباب باحثاً عن صحوته.

عن الإنسان فيكم أتحدث الآن.

فهو، لا ذاتكم الإلهية ولا القزم في الضباب، من يعرف الجريمة ويعرف العقاب.

غالباً ما سمعتكم تتحدثون عن مخطئ وكأنه ليس منكم، بل غريب عليكم، دخيل على عالمكم.

But I say that even as the holy and the righteous cannot rise beyond the highest which is in each of you,

So the wicked and the weak cannot fall lower than the lowest which is in you also.

And as a single leaf turns not yellow but with the silent knowledge of the whole tree,

So the wrong doer cannot do wrong without the hidden will of you all.

Like a procession you walk together towards your god-self.

You are the way and the wayfarers.

And when one of you falls down he falls for those behind him, a caution against the stumbling stone.

وأقول لكم، كما لا يستطيع التقي والصالح التعلّي
فوق الأعلى الذي في كل منكم،
فإن الخبيث والضعيف لا يهبطان دون الأدنى الذي
فيكم أيضاً.
وكما لا تؤول ورقة إلى اصفرار إلا بعلم الشجرة
الصامت،
فإن المخطئ لا يخطئ إلا بإرادتكم الخفية أجمعين.
مثل كوكبة إلى ذاتكم الإلهية تسيرون.
أنتم الطريق وأنتم العابرون.
وعندما يسقط أحدكم فإنما يسقط من أجل من وراءه،
تحذيراً له من العثرة أمامه.

Ay, and he falls for those ahead of him,
who though faster and surer of foot, yet
removed not the stumbling stone.

And this also, though the word lie heavy
upon your hearts:

The murdered is not unaccountable for
his own murder.

And the robbed is not blameless in being
robbed.

The righteous is not innocent of the
deeds of the wicked,

And the white-handed is not clean in the
doings of the felon.

Yea, the guilty is oftentimes the victim of
the injured.

أجل، ويسقط من أجل من سبقه، الذي رغم سرعته
وثقته الأكبر بخفته، لم يزِل عثرة الطريق.

وأقول هذا أيضاً، رغم كره ما سأقول:
ليس القتيل بحِل من جريمة قتله،
ليس من سرق ماله بطاهر الذيل في سرقة ماله.
ليس الصالح ببريء من أذيّة الخبيث،
ولا أبيض اليد بنظيف مما فعله الأثيم.
أجل، غالباً ما كان الجارح ضحية الجريح،

And still more often the condemned is the burden bearer for the guiltless and the unblamed.

You cannot separate the just from the unjust and the good from the wicked;

For they stand together before the face of the sun even as the black thread and the white are woven together.

And when the black thread breaks, the weaver shall look into the whole cloth, and he shall examine the loom also.

If any of you would bring to judgment the unfaithful wife,

Let him also weigh the heart of her husband in scales and measure his soul with measurements.

وأكثر منه المدان يحمل وزر من خرج غير ملوم وغير مذنب.

لا تستطيعون فصل الطيب عن الخبيث، ولا العادل عن الظالم؛

معاً يقفان في وجه الشمس، كخيط أسود وخيط أبيض بُرِما في رداء واحد.

فإذا ما انقطع الأسود، نظر الحائك في كامل الثوب وفحص النول كذلك.

وإن قاضى أحدكم زوجة خانت الإخلاص،
فليزن بالموازين قلب زوجها، وليقس بالمقاييس روحه.

And let him who would lash the offender look unto the spirit of the offended.

And if any of you would punish in the name of righteousness and lay the ax unto the evil tree, let him see to its roots;

And verily he will find the roots of the good and the bad, the fruitful and the fruitless, all entwined together in the silent heart of the earth.

And you judges who would be just,

What judgment pronounce you upon him who though honest in the flesh yet is a thief in spirit?

What penalty lay you upon him who slays in the flesh yet is himself slain in the spirit?

And how prosecute you him who in action is a deceiver and an oppressor,

ولينظر من سيجلد المعتدي في روح المعتدى عليه.

وإن عاقبتم باسم الحق وأنزلتم الفأس بجذع الشر،
فانظروا في الجذور؛

ولسوف ترون جذور الخير وجذور الشر، وجذور
الخصب وجذور العقم، بعضها لا مراء مجدول حول
بعض في قلب الأرض الصامت.

ويا أيها القضاة، يا من يناط بهم القصاص،

أي حد تقيمون على من كان أميناً في اللحم وسارقاً
في الروح؟

أي عقاب توقعون على من ذَبَح في اللحمِ وهو في
الروح ذبيح؟

كيف تحاكمون من خادع وقمع،

Yet who also is aggrieved and outraged?

And how shall you punish those whose remorse is already greater than their misdeeds?

Is not remorse the justice which is administered by the very law which you would fain serve?

Yet you cannot lay remorse upon the innocent nor lift it from the heart of the guilty.

Unbidden shall it call in the night, that men may wake and gaze upon themselves.

And you who would understand justice, how shall you unless you look upon all deeds in the fullness of light?

وهو محزون وفوق حدود الغضب غاضب؟

كيف تعاقبون من فاق ندمه ذنوبه؟
أليس الندم هو العدل يقيمه القانون الذي به تحكمون؟
لن تستطيعوا فرض الندم على بريء ولا رفعه عن
قلوب المذنبين.
في هزيع الليل يأتي بلا نداء، ليفيق رجال وبحالهم
يتفكرون.
وأنتم يا من تفهمون العدل، كيف تفهمونه إن لم
تنظروا الأعمال، كل الأعمال، في ذروة النور؟

Only then shall you know that the erect and the fallen are but one man standing in the twilight between the night of his pigmy-self and the day of his god-self,

And that the corner-stone of the temple is not higher than the lowest stone in its foundation.

حينها فقط ستعلمون أن السوي والساقط واحد يقف في الغسق بين نهار ذاته الإلهية وليل ذاته القزم، وأن حجر الزاوية في المعبد لا يعلو على أخفض حجر في أساسه.

THEN a lawyer said, But what of our **Laws**, master?

And he answered:

You delight in laying down laws,

You even delight more in breaking them.

Like children playing by the ocean who build sand towers with constancy and then destroy them with laughter.

But while you build your sand towers the ocean brings more sand to the shore,

And when you destroy them the ocean laughs with you.

Verily the ocean laughs always with the innocent.

But what of those to whom life is not an ocean, and man-made laws are not sand-towers,

ثم قال محام، ماذا عن **قوانيننا**، أيها المعلم؟

فأجاب:

يفرحكم سن القوانين،

لكنكم في مخالفتها أكثر تفرحون.

مثل أطفال على شاطئ البحر يلعبون، وبدأب يبنون أبراج رمل ويهدمون ما بنَوه ضاحكين.

وفيما تبنون الأبراج يحمل البحر من الرمل إلى الشاطئ المزيد،

وإذ تهدمون ما بنيتم يضحك البحر معكم.

هكذا البحر، دائماً يضحك كلما راح الأبرياء يضحكون.

لكن ماذا عن الذين لا يرون الحياة بحراً، ولا قوانين الإنسان أبراج رمل؟

But to whom life is a rock, and the law a chisel with which they would carve it in their own likeness?

What of the cripple who hates dancers?

What of the ox who loves his yoke and deems the elk and deer of the forest stray and vagrant things?

What of the old serpent who cannot shed his skin and calls all others naked and shameless?

And of him who comes early to the wedding-feast, and when over-fed and tired goes his way saying that all feasts are violation and all feasters lawbreakers?

الذين يرون الحياة صخرة، والقانون إزميلاً به ينحتون
منها على صورتهم تماثيل؟

ماذا عن القعيد يكره الراقصين؟

والثور ألِف نيره فحسب الوعِل وظبي الغابة أشياء
شاردة في التيه؟

وماذا عن الصِل الطاعن، لم يستطع طرح جلده
فوصم الحيات بالعري المشين؟

وماذا عن الذي خف إلى وليمة العرس قبل الموعد،
فإذا ما أتخم وتعب مضى ولسان حاله يقول، كل الولائم
ضلال وكل المحتفلين مارقون؟

What shall I say of these save that they too stand in the sunlight, but with their backs to the sun?

They see only their shadows, and their shadows are their laws.

And what is the sun to them but a caster of shadows?

And what is it to acknowledge the laws but to stoop down and trace their shadows upon the earth?

But you who walk facing the sun, what images drawn on the earth can hold you?

You who travel with the wind, what weather-vane shall direct your course?

What man's law shall bind you if you break your yoke but upon no man's prison door?

ماذا عن هؤلاء غير أنهم في ضوء الشمس كذلك واقفون، لكنهم للشمس ظهورهم يديرون؟

لا يرون إلا ظلالهم، وظلالهم لهم القانون.

وهل الشمس لهؤلاء إلا مذرّة ظلال؟

وهل اعترافهم بالقوانين إلا انحناء وتعقب لظلالهم على الأديم؟

لكنكم، يا من تولون وجوهكم الشمس، أي أخيلة على الأرض مرسومة تكفيكم أمركم؟

ويا أيها المسافرون مع الريح، أية دوارة ريح توجه دربكم؟

أي قانون لبشر يلزِمكم إن حطمتم قيدكم ولم تحطموه على باب سِجن إنسان؟

What laws shall you fear if you dance but stumble against no man's iron chains?

And who is he that shall bring you to judgment if you tear off your garment yet leave it in no man's path?

People of Orphalese, you can muffle the drum, and you can loosen the strings of the lyre, but who shall command the skylark not to sing?

أي قانون يرهبكم إن رقصتم ولم تعثروا بأغلال إنسان؟

ومن سيحاكمكم إن مزقتم ثوبكم ولم تتركوه في درب إنسان؟

يا أهل أورفليس، تستطيعون كتم أصوات الطبول، وحل أوتار القيثار، لكن هل من يقدر على أن يمنع القبّرة عن الغناء مع الأطيار؟

AND an orator said, Speak to us of **Freedom**,

And he answered:

At the city gate and by your fireside I have seen you prostrate yourself and worship your own freedom,

Even as slaves humble themselves before a tyrant and praise him though he slays them.

Ay, in the grove of the temple and in the shadow of the citadel I have seen the freest among you wear their freedom as a yoke and a handcuff.

And my heart bled within me; for you can only be free when even the desire of seeking freedom becomes a harness to you, and when you cease to speak of freedom as a goal and a fulfilment.

وقال خطيب، حدثنا عن **الحرية**،

فأجاب:

بباب المدينة وجانب الموقد رأيتكم ساجدين وحريتكم تعبدون،

مثل أرقاء لطاغية يتذللون، ويذهبون في مدحه وهم على يديه يذبحون.

بلى، وفي غيضة المعبد وظل القلعة، رأيت أكثركم عتقاً يلبس حريته كقيد ونير.

ونزف القلب مني؛ فلن تكونوا أحراراً حتى يصبح شوق البحث عن الحرية ذاته قيداً، وتكفوا عن ذكرها كهدف وإنجاز كبير.

You shall be free indeed when your days are not without a care nor your nights without a want and a grief,

But rather when these things girdle your life and yet you rise above them naked and unbound.

And how shall you rise beyond your days and nights unless you break the chains which you at the dawn of your understanding have fastened around your noon hour?

In truth that which you call freedom is the strongest of these chains, though its links glitter in the sun and dazzle your eyes.

أحراراً تكونون حين لا تخلو أيامكم من هم ولياليكم من عوَز وغم،

بل عندما تطوق هذه حياتكم وتسمون فوقها عراة طلقاء.

وكيف تعلون فوق أيامكم ولياليكم، ما لم تحطموا القيد الذي في فجر فهمكم أوثقتم به نهاركم؟

هذه التي تسمونها الحرية هي أقوى القيود، رغم لمعان حلقاتها في الشمس وإبهارها العيون.

And what is it but fragments of your own self you would discard that you may become free?

If it is an unjust law you would abolish, that law was written with your own hand upon your own forehead.

You cannot erase it by burning your law books nor by washing the foreheads of your judges, though you pour the sea upon them.

And if it is a despot you would dethrone, see first that his throne erected within you is destroyed.

For how can a tyrant rule the free and the proud, but for a tyranny in their own freedom and a shame in their own pride?

وهل ما ستتبذونه كي تصبحوا أحراراً إلا نتفاً من
ذاتكم؟

فإذا كان ما تريدون إلغاءه قانوناً جائراً، فأنتم من بيده
خط على جبينه القانون.

لن تستطيعوا محوه بحرق كتب قوانينكم ولا بغسل
جباه قضاتكم، وإن صببتم عليها البحر.

وإذا كان طاغية تريدون خلعه، فحطموا أولاً عرشه
المقام بداخلكم.

فكيف يحكم الأحرار الأباة طاغية، إن لم يكن في
حريتهم هناك طغيان، وعار في كرامتهم؟

And if it is a care you would cast off, that care has been chosen by you rather than imposed upon you.

And if it is a fear you would dispel, the seat of that fear is in your heart and not in the hand of the feared.

Verily all things move within your being in constant half embrace, the desired and the dreaded, the repugnant and the cherished, the pursued and that which you would escape.

These things move within you as lights and shadows in pairs that cling.

And when the shadow fades and is no more, the light that lingers becomes a shadow to another light.

وإذا كان همّاً ما تريدون نبذه، فأنتم من اختار الهم والهم لم يفرض عليكم.

وإذا كان خوفاً ما تريدون طرده، فالخوف في قلوبكم لا بيد من تخافون.

ألا في شبه عناق دائم تمور في كيانك الأشياء، كل الأشياء؛ ما ترهبه وما تتلهف له، ما تأباه وما تميل إليه، ما تنشده وما تروم خلاصاً منه.

أشياء تتحرك فيك، قرينين متلاصقين تلاصق الظل والنور.

فإن خبا وغابِ الظل، بات النور المتبطئ ظلاً لنور.

And thus your freedom when it loses its fetters becomes itself the fetter of a greater freedom.

وهكذا حريتك، ما أن تفقد قيدها حتى تصبح ذاتها قيداً لحرية أعظم وعتق كبير.

AND the priestess spoke again and said:
Speak to us of **Reason and Passion**.

And he answered, saying:

Your soul is oftentimes a battlefield, upon
which your reason and your judgment
wage war against your passion and your
appetite.

Would that I could be the peacemaker in
your soul, that I might turn the discord and
the rivalry of your elements into oneness
and melody.

But how shall I, unless you yourselves be
also the peacemakers, nay, the lovers of all
your elements?

Your reason and your passion are the
rudder and the sails of your seafaring soul.

وتكلمت الكاهنة ثانية وقالت، حدثنا عن **العاطفة والعقل،**

فأجاب، قائلاً:

غالباً ما كانت روحكم معتركاً في ساحه يشن عقلكم وحكمكم حرباً على عاطفتكم وعلى ما تشتهون.

ليتني كنت صانع السلام في روحكم، لأحيل تنافر وتنافس عناصركم إلى وحدة ولحن جميل.

لكن كيف لي، ما لم تكونوا أنتم كذلك صناع السلام، ولجميع عناصركم محبين؟

عقلكم وعاطفتكم لروحكم المبحرة دفة وهما لها شراع.

If either your sails or your rudder be broken, you can but toss and drift, or else be held at a standstill in mid-seas.

For reason, ruling alone, is a force confining; and passion, unattended is a flame that burns to its own destruction.

Therefore let your soul exalt your reason to the height of passion, that it may sing;

And let it direct your passion with reason, that your passion may live through its own daily resurrection, and like the phoenix rise above its own ashes.

I would have you consider your judgment and your appetite even as you would two loved guests in your house.

فإذا انكسرت الدفة أو تحطم الشراع، فالانجراف وتقاذف الموج، أو الحصار في البحار بلا حراك.

فالعقل، إذا انفرد واستبد، قوة مقيدة؛ والعاطفة، إن فقدت الرقيب، نار تأكل بعضها حتى الهلاك.

فدعوا الروح تسمو بالعقل إلى ذرى العاطفة، ليصدح؛ وتوجه العاطفة بالعقل، لتحيا العاطفة بعد موت كل يوم، ومن رمادها تنهض كالعنقاء.

ليتكم تنظرون لحكمكم وشاهيتكم نظرتكم لحبيبين حلا بكم ضيفين.

Surely you would not honour one guest above the other; for he who is more mindful of one loses the love and the faith of both.

Among the hills, when you sit in the cool shade of the white poplars, sharing the peace and serenity of distant fields and meadows– then let your heart say in silence, 'God rests in reason.'

And when the storm comes, and the mighty wind shakes the forest and thunder and lightning proclaim the majesty of the sky,– then let your heart say in awe, 'God moves in passion.'

And since you are a breath in God's sphere, and a leaf in God's forest, you too should rest in reason and move in passion.

لن تكرموا ضيفاً على ضيف؛ فمن زاد الاحتفاء بواحد خسر محبة وإخلاص الاثنين.

عندما في فيء الحور الندي بين التلال تجلسون، وتتقاسمون السلام والسكينة مع المروج ونائي الحقول،- دعوا قلوبكم بصمت تقول، 'في العقل يستريح الله.'

وعندما تقبل العاصفة، وتهز الريح العاتية الغابة ويعلن البرق والرعد سلطة السماء،- دعوا قلوبكم في الروع تقول، 'في العاطفة يتحرك الله.'

ولأنكِ في دنيا الله نفحة، وورقة في غابة الله، فحتم أيضاً عليك أن تتحركي في العاطفة وتستريحي في العقل.

AND a woman spoke, saying, Tell us of
Pain.

And he said:

Your pain is the breaking of the shell that
encloses your understanding.

Even as the stone of the fruit must break,
that its heart may stand in the sun, so must
you know pain.

And could you keep your heart in
wonder at the daily miracles of your life,
your pain would not seem less wondrous
than your joy;

And you would accept the seasons of
your heart, even as you have always
accepted the seasons that pass over your
fields.

And you would watch with serenity
through the winters of your grief.

وتكلمت امرأة، وقالت، أخبرنا عن **الألم**،

فقال:

ألمكم هو انكسار القوقعة التي تطوق فهمكم.

وكما على نواة الثمرة أن تنفلق ليشرئب قلبها في الشمس، عليكم اختبار الألم.

ولو استطعتم إبقاء قلوبكم في دهَش أمام معجزات حياتكم تتبدى كل يوم، لأمِنتم إلى أن ألمكم لا يقل دهَشاً عن فرحكم؛

ولقبلتم بمواسم قلوبكم قَبولكم تعاقب الفصول على حقولكم.

ولرقبتم بهدوء وصفو تعاقب شتاء حزنكم.

Much of your pain is self-chosen.

It is the bitter potion by which the physician within you heals your sick self.

Therefore trust the physician, and drink his remedy in silence and tranquillity:

For his hand, though heavy and hard, is guided by the tender hand of the Unseen,

And the cup he brings, though it burns your lips, has been fashioned of the clay which the Potter has moistened with his own sacred tears.

ألمكم كثيره اختياركم.

هو الدواء المر به يشفي الطبيب فيكم عليل ذاتكم.

آمنوا بالطبيب، وارشفوا دواءه بسكون وصمت:

فيده، رغم ثقلها وبأسها، يوجهها الرؤوف الذي لا تراه عيونكم،

والكأس الذي يأتي به، رغم حرقه شفاهكم، قدّ من الطين الذي بطاهر دمعه بللَه صانعه.

AND a man said, Speak to us of **Self–knowledge**.

And he answered, saying:

Your hearts know in silence the secrets of the days and the nights.

But your ears thirst for the sound of your heart's knowledge.

You would know in words that which you have always known in thought.

You would touch with your fingers the naked body of your dreams.

And it is well you should.

The hidden well–spring of your soul must needs rise and run murmuring to the sea;

And the treasure of your infinite depths would be revealed to your eyes.

وقال رجل، حدثنا عن **معرفة النفس**،

فأجاب، قائلاً:

قلوبكم تعلم سر الأيام والليالي في صمت.

وآذانكم تهفو لسماع ما يعلمه القلب.

تريدون أن تعرفوا بالكلام ما تدركونه باللب.

وأن تلمسوا جسد أحلامكم العاري بأصابع اليد.

ويا لحسن ما تريدون.

ينبوع روحكم الخفي قدره أن يصعد ويجري رقراقاً لليم؛

فترى عيونكم كنوز أعماقكم التي ليس لعمقها حد.

But let there be no scales to weigh your unknown treasure;

And seek not the depths of your knowledge with staff or sounding line.

For self is a sea boundless and measureless.

Say not, 'I have found the truth,' but rather, 'I have found a truth.'

Say not, 'I have found the path of the soul.' Say rather, 'I have met the soul walking upon my path.'

For the soul walks upon all paths.

The soul walks not upon a line, neither does it grow like a reed.

The soul unfolds itself, like a lotus of countless petals.

لكن لا تجعلوا موازين لوزن كنزكم الذي لم تبصروه بعد؛

ولا تحاولوا سبر علمكم بعَصا أو مِرنان.

فالنفس يم بلا حد ولا أمد.

لا تقل، 'وجدت الحقيقة،' بل، 'حقيقةً وجدت.'

لا تقل، 'وجدت طريق الروح،' بل، 'الروحَ على دربي التقيت.'

إنما الروح على كل درب.

لا تتبع صراطاً، ولا تنمو كعود قصب.

تتفتح الروح كزهرة لوتُسٍ ليس لأوراقها عدد.

THEN said a teacher, Speak to us of **Teaching**.

And he said:

No man can reveal to you aught but that which already lies half asleep in the dawning of your knowledge.

The teacher who walks in the shadow of the temple, among his followers, gives not of his wisdom but rather of his faith and his lovingness.

If he is indeed wise he does not bid you enter the house of his wisdom, but rather leads you to the threshold of your own mind.

The astronomer may speak to you of his understanding of space, but he cannot give you his understanding.

ثم قال معلم، حدثنا عن **التعليم**،

فقال:

لا يقدِر امرؤ أن يكشف لك عما لا يرقد نصف نائم في فجر علمك.

المعلم الذي يطوف بظل المعبد بين أتباعه، لا يقدم من حكمته، بل من إيمانه ومحبته.

فلو أوتي الحكمة حقاً لقادك إلى تخوم عقلك، لا إلى دار حكمته.

قد يحدثك الفلكي عن فهمه للفضاء، لكنه لا يعطيك فهمه.

The musician may sing to you of the rhythm which is in all space, but he cannot give you the ear which arrests the rhythm nor the voice that echoes it.

And he who is versed in the science of numbers can tell of the regions of weight and measure, but he cannot conduct you thither.

For the vision of one man lends not its wings to another man.

And even as each one of you stands alone in God's knowledge, so must each one of you be alone in his knowledge of God and in his understanding of the earth.

قد يغني من إيقاع الكون لك المغني، لكنه لا يعطيك الأذن التي تلتقط الإيقاع ولا الصوت الذي يردده.

والبارع في علم الأرقام قادر على تفسير حقول الوزن والقياس، لكنه لا يقودك لعلمه.

فرؤية يملكها إنسان لا تعِير جناحها لغيره.

ومثلما تقف في علم الله وحيداً، عليك أن تكون كذلك وحيداً في علمك بالله وفهمك لخلقه.

AND a youth said, Speak to us of
Friendship.

And he answered, saying:

Your friend is your needs answered.

He is your field which you sow with love
and reap with thanksgiving.

And he is your board and your fireside.

For you come to him with your hunger
and you seek him for peace.

When your friend speaks his mind you
fear not the 'nay' in your own mind, nor
do you withhold the 'ay.'

And when he is silent your heart ceases
not to listen to his heart;

وقال شاب، حدثنا عن الصداقة،

فأجاب:

صديقك هو ري حاجاتك.

حقلك بالحب تزرعه وبالشكر تجني حصاده.

وهو مائدتك وجانب-نارك.

بجوعك تقصده وللأمان تذهب إلى أمانه.

عندما يقول صديقك رأيه، فأنت لا تخشى في ذهنك
قول 'لا،' ولا تعرض عن قول 'نعم.'

وإذا صمت، لا يتوقف قلبك عن الإصغاء إلى جنانه؛

151

For without words, in friendship, all thoughts, all desires, all expectations are born and shared, with joy that is unacclaimed.

When you part from your friend, you grieve not;

For that which you love most in him may be clearer in his absence, as the mountain to the climber is clearer from the plain.

And let there be no purpose in friendship save the deepening of the spirit.

For love that seeks aught but the disclosure of its own mystery is not love but a net cast forth: and only the unprofitable is caught.

And let your best be for your friend.

في الصداقة، تولد الرغائب، والأفكار، والآمال كلها بلا كلام ويتقاسمها الصديق مع الصديق، بفرح غير مُهلِّل.

عندما تفارق صديقك، فأنت لا تحزن؛
فجلّ ما أحببت فيه ربما كان أكثر جلاء في غيابه، كما الجبل للمتسلق أكثر وضوحاً من السهل منه في اقترابه.
ولا تجعل للصداقة من غاية سوى تعميق الروح.
فحب لا يكشف سره ليس حباً، بل شبكة ترمى: ولا تصيد إلا الشوائب.

واحتفظ لصديقك بأحسنِك.

If he must know the ebb of your tide, let him know its flood also.

For what is your friend that you should seek him with hours to kill?

Seek him always with hours to live.

For it is his to fill your need, but not your emptiness.

And in the sweetness of friendship let there be laughter, and sharing of pleasures.

For in the dew of little things the heart finds its morning and is refreshed.

فإن لم يكن من علمه بانحسار مدك بدٌ، فدعه يعلم أيضاً بطوفانه.

فمن تظن صفيك حتى تقصده لقتل ساعات زمانك؟

صفيك دائماً اقصده كي تعيش ساعات زمانك.

فهو من يملأ حاجتك، لا فراغك.

وفي نعيم الود خلّ هناك ضحكات، وتقاسماً للمسرة.

فالقلب يرى صباحه وهناءه في ندى الأشياء والذوائب.

AND then a scholar said, Speak of **Talking**.

And he answered, saying:

You talk when you cease to be at peace with your thoughts;

And when you can no longer dwell in the solitude of your heart you live in your lips, and sound is a diversion and a pastime.

And in much of your talking, thinking is half murdered.

For thought is a bird of space, that in a cage of words may indeed unfold its wings but cannot fly.

There are those among you who seek the talkative through fear of being alone.

ثم قال عالم، حدثنا عن **الكلام**،

فأجاب:

تتكلمونَ إذ مع أفكاركم تفقدون الوئام؛

وعندما في عزلة قلوبكم تعافون العيش إلى شفاهكم ينتقل المقام، فالصوت تسلية والنبرة انسجام.

في كثير كلامكم، يُزهَق التفكير أو يكاد،

فالفكر طائر فضاء، قد يفرد الجناح في قفص الكلام لكنه لا يحلق.

هناك من يلوذ بالهذر خوفاً من الوحدة.

The silence of aloneness reveals to their eyes their naked selves and they would escape.

And there are those who talk, and without knowledge or forethought reveal a truth which they themselves do not understand.

And there are those who have the truth within them, but they tell it not in words.

In the bosom of such as these the spirit dwells in rhythmic silence.

When you meet your friend on the roadside or in the market place, let the spirit in you move your lips and direct your tongue.

Let the voice within your voice speak to the ear of his ear;

صمت الوحدة يعري حقيقتهم لعيونهم فيهربون.

وهناك من يتكلم، ومن غير أن يدري يكشف عن حقيقة لا يعيها.

وهناك من يحيط بالحقيقة، ولا يفصح عنها.

بصدر هؤلاء ترفل الروح في إيقاع صامت.

عندما على قارعة الطريق أو في ساحة السوق تلقى الصديق، دع الروح فيك تحرك شفتيك وتوجه لسانك، ودع الصوت الذي داخل صوتك يخاطب الأذن التي داخل أذنه؛

For his soul will keep the truth of your
heart as the taste of the wine is remembered
When the colour is forgotten and the
vessel is no more.

فروحه تحفظ حقيقة قلبك مثلما تحفظ الذاكرة للنبيذ مذاقه

عندما ننسى لونه ونفقد وعاءه.

AND an astronomer said, Master, what of **Time**?

And he answered:

You would measure time the measureless and the immeasurable.

You would adjust your conduct and even direct the course of your spirit according to hours and seasons.

Of time you would make a stream upon whose bank you would sit and watch its flowing.

Yet the timeless in you is aware of life's timelessness,

And knows that yesterday is but today's memory and tomorrow is today's dream.

وقال فلكي، ماذا عن **الزمن**، يا سيدي؟

فأجاب:

تريدون أن تقيسوا الزمن الذي لا يحد ولا يقاس،

وأن تلائموا سلوككم، وتوجهوا حتى روحكم بالفصول وبالساعات،

وتجعلوا من الزمن جدولاً تجلسون على ضفافه وتراقبون انسيابه.

لكن السرمدي فيكم يعي السرمدي في الحياة،

ويدرك أن الأمس لليوم ذكرى وأن الغد حلم النهار،

And that that which sings and contemplates in you is still dwelling within the bounds of that first moment which scattered the stars into space.

Who among you does not feel that his power to love is boundless?

And yet who does not feel that very love, though boundless, encompassed within the centre of his being, and moving not from love thought to love thought, nor from love deeds to other love deeds?

And is not time even as love is, undivided and paceless?

But if in your thought you must measure time into seasons, let each season encircle all the other seasons,

وأن الشادي المتأمل فيكم مازال أسير اللحظة التي نثرت النجوم في الفضاء.

من منكم لا يشعر أن قدرته على الحب قدرة بلا حد؟

ومن ذا الذي لا يشعر بعين ذاك الحب، رغم لانهائيته، كامناً في سويدائه، لا يتنقل من فكرة حب إلى فكرة حب، ولا من مآثر حب إلى مآثر حب؟

أوليس الزمن إذن كالحب، لا قسمة ولا خطى له؟

لكن إن لم يكن من قياس الزمن في ذهنك بد ومن تقسيمه إلى فصول، فدع كل فصل يضم باقي الفصول،

And let today embrace the past with remembrance and the future with longing.

ودع الحاضر يعانق الماضي بالتذكر، والمستقبل
بالشوق.

AND one of the elders of the city said, Speak to us of **Good and Evil**.

And he answered:

Of the good in you I can speak, but not of the evil.

For what is evil but good tortured by its own hunger and thirst?

Verily when good is hungry it seeks food even in dark caves, and when it thirsts it drinks even of dead waters.

You are good when you are one with yourself.

Yet when you are not one with yourself you are not evil.

For a divided house is not a den of thieves; it is only a divided house.

وقال كهل من المدينة، حدثنا عن **الخير والشر**،
فأجاب:

عن الخير فيكم، لا عن الشر أستطيع الكلام.

وهل الشر إلا خير عذبه عطشه وأضناه جوعه؟

إذا ما الخير جاع، فتش عن القوت في كهوف
الظلام، وإذا ظمئ شرب حتى من الماء الحرام.

أنت خير عندما تكون ونفسك واحداً،

ولست شراً عندما لا تكون ونفسك واحداً.

فمنزل مقسم ليس وكراً للصوص؛ هو منزل مقسم لا
غير.

And a ship without rudder may wander aimlessly among perilous isles yet sink not to the bottom.

You are good when you strive to give of yourself.

Yet you are not evil when you seek gain for yourself.

For when you strive for gain you are but a root that clings to the earth and sucks at her breast.

Surely the fruit cannot say to the root, 'Be like me, ripe and full and ever giving of your abundance.'

For to the fruit giving is a need, and receiving is a need to the root.

وقد تتيه بين جزر المخاطر بلا دفة سفينة ولا تغرق في قاع البحور.

أنت خير إذ تجهد للعطاء من ذاتك
ولست شراً إذ تبحث عن كسب لذاتك.
ما أنت في سعيك للأخذ إلا جذر تشبث بالثرى
يرضع من ثدي الأرض.
لن تقول الثمرة للجذر، 'كن مثلي، ناضجاً ريان، أبداً
تعطي من وفرك وفيضك.'
فالعطاء للثمرة حاجة، والأخذ حاجة للجذور.

You are good when you are fully awake in your speech.

Yet you are not evil when you sleep while your tongue staggers without purpose.

And even stumbling speech may strengthen a weak tongue.

You are good when you walk to your goal firmly and with bold steps.

Yet you are not evil when you go thither limping.

For those who limp go not backward.

But you who are strong and swift, see that you do not limp before the lame, deeming it kindness.

أنت خير عندما تتكلم صاحياً،

ولست شراً عندما تنام ولسانك يرطن بلا جدوى.

فلكم من لسان ضعيف صار بعاثر القول أقوى.

أنت خير في سيركَ إلى غايتك ثابتاً غير هياب.

ولست شراً إذا سرت بخطى عرجاء.

حتى الذي في مشيه عرج لا يسير إلى وراء.

وأنت، يا من تملك القوة والخفة، حاذر العرج أمام

أعرج، ظناً ذلك لطفاً.

You are good in countless ways and you are not evil when you are not good.

You are only loitering and sluggard.

Pity that the stags cannot teach swiftness to the turtles.

In your longing for your giant self lies your goodness: and that longing is in all of you.

But in some of you that longing is a torrent rushing with might to the sea, carrying the secrets of the hillsides and the songs of the forest.

And in others it is a flat stream that loses itself in angles and bends and lingers before it reaches the shore.

أنت خير في ألف حالة وحالة ولست شراً عندما لا
تكون خيراً،
ما أنت إلا مبَطئ يسير في أناة.
لا يستطيع الأُيَّل، وأسفي، أن يعلم الخفة للسُلَحفاة.

في توقكم لذاتكم الكبرى خيركم: هو توق في كل
منكم.
وهو عند نفر سيل يهدر نحو البحر، حاملاً أسرار
التلال وأغاني الغابة.
وعند نفر وشَلٌ شتته المنعطف وضيعه المنحنى،
مهلاً ينساب قبل وصوله الشاطئ.

But let not him who longs much say to him who longs little, 'Wherefore are you slow and halting?'

For the truly good ask not the naked, 'Where is your garment?' nor the houseless, 'What has befallen your house?'

ولا تدع كثير الشوق يقول لقليله، 'لماذا التعثر ولماذا التباطؤ؟'

فالصادق من أهل الخير لا يسأل العاري، 'أين ثيابك؟' ولا الشريد، 'ماذا حل بمنزلك؟'

THEN a priestess said, Speak to us of
Prayer.

And he answered, saying:

You pray in your distress and in your
need; would that you might pray also in the
fullness of your joy and in your days of
abundance.

For what is prayer but the expansion of
yourself into the living ether?

And if it is for your comfort to pour your
darkness into space, it is also for your
delight to pour forth the dawning of your
heart.

And if you cannot but weep when your
soul summons you to prayer, she should
spur you again and yet again, though
weeping, until you shall come laughing.

ثم قالت كاهنة، حدثنا عن **الصلاة**،

فقال:

في شقائكم وعند حاجتكم تصلون؛ وليتكم في عز فرحكم وأوج رخائكم كذلك صليتم.

فما عسى الصلاة أن تكون غير امتداد ذاتكِ في الأثير؟

فإن وجدتِ في سكب ليلك في الفضاء راحة، فلسوف يبهجك أيضاً أن تسكبي فجر قلبك فيه.

وإن لم تملكي إذ تدعوك روحك للصلاة حبس العبرات، فلسوف تهيج الصلاة بك مرات، حتى إذا بك رغم نحيبك تضحكين.

When you pray you rise to meet in the air those who are praying at that very hour, and whom save in prayer you may not meet.

Therefore let your visit to that temple invisible be for naught but ecstasy and sweet communion.

For if you should enter the temple for no other purpose than asking you shall not receive.

And if you should enter into it to humble yourself you shall not be lifted.

Or even if you should enter into it to beg for the good of others you shall not be heard.

It is enough that you enter the temple invisible.

عندما تصلين تصعدين لتلقي الذين ذات الساعة في الهواء يصلون، الذين لولا الصلاة لما التقيت.

فلا تجعلي لزيارتك معبد الغيب من غاية سوى النشوة وحلاوة الجمع.

فإذا ما دخلت المعبد لا تبغين إلا الطلب لما جُبِرتِ.

وإن دخلته خافضة جناح الذل من التواضع لما رُفِعتِ.

وحتى إذا دخلته مستجدية الخير للناس لما سُمِعتِ.

يكفيك أنك في معبد الغيب.

I cannot teach you how to pray in words.

God listens not to your words save when He Himself utters them through your lips.

And I cannot teach you the prayer of the seas and the forests and the mountains.

But you who are born of the forests and the mountains and the seas can find their prayer in your heart,

And if you but listen in the stillness of the night you shall hear them saying in silence:

'Our God who art our winged self, it is thy will in us that willeth.

It is thy desire in us that desireth.

It is thy urge in us that would turn our nights, which are thine, into days which are thine also.

لا أستطيع أن أعلمك الصلاة بالكلمات.

فالله لا يصغي لكلماتك حتى تبثها ذاته عبر شفتيك.

ولا أستطيع أن أعلمك صلاة البحار والغابات والجبال.

لكنكم يا مَن ولدتم مِن رحم البحار والجبال والغابات، في قلوبكم تجدون صلاتها،

وإن أنتم في هدأة الليل أصغيتم لسمعتموها في صمت تقول،

'ربنا يا من لنا الذات والجناح، مشيئتك فينا هي التي تشاء.

شوقك فينا هو الذي يشتاق.

دافعك فينا هو الذي سيحيل ليلنا، وهو ملكك، نهاراً هو ملكك أيضاً.

We cannot ask thee for aught, for thou knowest our needs before they are born in us:

Thou art our need; and in giving us more of thyself thou givest us all.'

لا نملك أن نسألك شيئاً، فأنت عالم بحاجاتنا قبل أن تولد فينا الحاجات:

أنت حاجتنا؛ وبعطائك المزيد من ذاتك لنا تهبنا كل شيء..،

THEN a hermit, who visited the city once a year, came forth and said, Speak to us of **Pleasure**.

And he answered, saying:

Pleasure is a freedom-song,

But it is not freedom.

It is the blossoming of your desires,

But it is not their fruit.

It is a depth calling unto a height,

But it is not the deep nor the high.

It is the caged taking wing,

But it is not space encompassed.

Ay, in very truth, pleasure is a freedom-song.

And I fain would have you sing it with fullness of heart; yet I would not have you lose your hearts in the singing.

ثم تقدم ناسك يزور المدينة مرة في العام، وقال، حدثنا
في **المتعة**،

فأجاب:

المتعة أنشودة حرية،

لكنها ليست الحرية.

هي براعم شوقك في تفتحها،

وليست ثمرة الأشواق.

هي غور ينادي علاء،

لكنها ليست الغور ولا هي العلاء.

هي الحبيس صفق الجناح،

لا فضاء يحيطه فضاء.

بلى، وقول الحق، المتعة أنشودة حرية.

ليتكم تغنونها ملء شغافكم؛ ولا تفقدون قلوبكم في
الغناء.

Some of your youth seek pleasure as if it were all, and they are judged and rebuked.

I would not judge nor rebuke them. I would have them seek.

For they shall find pleasure, but not her alone;

Seven are her sisters, and the least of them is more beautiful than pleasure.

Have you not heard of the man who was digging in the earth for roots and found a treasure?

And some of your elders remember pleasures with regret like wrongs committed in drunkenness.

But regret is the beclouding of the mind and not its chastisement.

188

بعض شبابكم يبحث عن المتعة كأنها كل الأشياء، فيحاكمون ويعنفون.

أنا لن أحاكمهم ولن أعنفهم. سأتركهم في بحثهم ماضين.

ولسوف يجدون المتعة، لكن ليس المتعة وحدها يجدون.

سبعٌ أخواتها، أقلها أكثر جمالاً من المتعة.

أما سمعتم بالذي وجد كنزاً وهو ينبش باحثاً عن جذور؟

وبعض شيوخكم يستذكر اللذات بتندم كخطايا ارتكبت في سِكر.

أما التندم فسحابة تغشى العقل لا عقاب للعقل.

189

They should remember their pleasures with gratitude, as they would the harvest of a summer.

Yet if it comforts them to regret, let them be comforted.

And there are among you those who are not young to seek nor old to remember;

And in their fear of seeking and remembering they shun all pleasures, lest they neglect the spirit or offend against it.

But even in their foregoing is their pleasure.

And thus they too find pleasure though they dig for roots with quivering hands.

But tell me, who is he that can offend the spirit?

فليستذكروا لذاتهم بامتنان، تذكَرَهم حصادَ صيف،
وإن أراحهم أن يتندموا، فهم وما إليه يرتاحون.

وبينكم من هم ليسوا شباباً للبحث ولا شيوخاً للتذكر؛
في خوفهم من البحث والتذكر يتجنبون اللذات كلها،
خشية إهمال أو إساءة للروح.
لكنهم حتى في تفويتهم المتعة يجدون متعة.
ويجدون هم كذلك كنزاً رغم بحثهم بارتعاش عن
الجذور.
لكن، حلفتكم، من يقدر أن يسيء للروح؟

Shall the nightingale offend the stillness of the night, or the firefly the stars?

And shall your flame or your smoke burden the wind?

Think you the spirit is a still pool which you can trouble with a staff?

Oftentimes in denying yourself pleasure you do but store the desire in the recesses of your being.

Who knows but that which seems omitted today, waits for tomorrow?

For your body knows its heritage and its rightful need and will not be deceived.

And your body is the harp of your soul,

And it is yours to bring forth sweet music from it or confused sounds.

هل يخدش العندليب سكون الليل، أو اليراعة النجوم؟

هل يرهق لهيبك أو دخانك الريح؟

هل تحسب الروح بركة ماء راكد وأنك تعكر الماء بعود؟

بإنكاركم المتعة على أنفسكم تغيّبون الرغبة في الكيان.

ومن يعلم أن ما يبدو قد أُسقِط اليومَ، لا ينتظر أن يعود؟

جسدك يدرك إرثه وحق حاجته، ولن يقبل خداعه.

وهو قيثارة روحك،

ولك أن تأخذ ناشز الأصوات منه أو من الألحان الحلو.

And now you ask in your heart, 'How shall we distinguish that which is good in pleasure from that which is not good?'

Go to your fields and your gardens, and you shall learn that it is the pleasure of the bee to gather honey of the flower,

But it is also the pleasure of the flower to yield its honey to the bee.

For to the bee a flower is a fountain of life,

And to the flower a bee is a messenger of love,

And to both, bee and flower, the giving and the receiving of pleasure is a need and an ecstasy.

People of Orphalese, be in your pleasures like the flowers and the bees.

والآن في قلوبكم تسألون، 'كيف نفرق في المتعة بين
ما هو خير وما ليس بخير؟'

اخرجوا إلى حقولكم وحدائقكم، ولسوف ترون أن جني
العسل من الزهرة متعة النحلة،

وأن طرح العسل للنحلة متعة الزهرة.

فالزهرة للنحلة ينبوع حياة،

والنحلة للزهرة رسول حب،

ولسوف ترون أن عطاء المتعة وأخذها، لكليهما،
النحلة والزهرة، حاجة وسرور .

يا معشر أورفليس، كونوا في لذاتكم مثل النحل
ومثل الزهور .

AND a poet said, Speak to us of **Beauty**.

And he answered:

Where shall you seek beauty, and how shall you find her unless she herself be your way and your guide?

And how shall you speak of her except she be the weaver of your speech?

The aggrieved and the injured say, 'Beauty is kind and gentle.

Like a young mother half-shy of her own glory she walks among us.'

And the passionate say, 'Nay, beauty is a thing of might and dread.

Like the tempest she shakes the earth beneath us and the sky above us.'

وقال شاعر، حدثنا عن الجمال،

فأجاب:

أين تطلبون الجمال، وكيف تجدونه إن لم يكن ذاته الطريق والدليل؟

وكيف تتحدثون عنه إن لم ينسج هو الحديث؟

يقول المحزون والمكلوم، 'اَلجمال رقيق ولطيف.

كأم صغيرة حيية بعزها بيننا يسير.'

ويقول الهائج والجموح، 'كلا، الجمال رهبة وجبروت.

كالإعصار يهز الأرض من تحتنا ويرعش السماء من فوق.'

The tired and the weary say, 'Beauty is of soft whisperings. She speaks in our spirit.

Her voice yields to our silences like a faint light that quivers in fear of the shadow.'

But the restless say, 'We have heard her shouting among the mountains,

And with her cries came the sound of hoofs, and the beating of wings and the roaring of lions.'

At night the watchmen of the city say, 'Beauty shall rise with the dawn from the east.'

ويقول المتعب والملول، 'الجمال عذب الهمس. يتكلم في الروح.

صوته يراعي سكناتنا كنور خافت يرعَش خائفاً من الظل.'

لكن الجزِع الهلِع يقول، 'سمعت الجمال بين الجبال يصيح،

ومع الصياح صوت حوافر، وصفق أجنحة وزئير أسود.'

في الليل يقول حراس المدينة، 'سيطلع الجمال من شرقٍ مع انبلاج الصبح.'

And at noontide the toilers and the wayfarers say, 'We have seen her leaning over the earth from the windows of the sunset.'

In winter say the snow-bound, 'She shall come with the spring leaping upon the hills.'

And in the summer heat the reapers say, 'We have seen her dancing with the autumn leaves, and we saw a drift of snow in her hair.'

All these things have you said of beauty,

Yet in truth you spoke not of her but of needs unsatisfied,

And beauty is not a need but an ecstasy.

It is not a mouth thirsting nor an empty hand stretched forth,

وفي الظهيرة يقول الكادح وعابر السبيل، 'رأيناه متكئاً
على الأديم من شُرَف الغروب.'

في الشتاء يقول الخارجون للثلج، 'سيأتي الجمال
على التلال وثباً مع الربيع.'

وفي حر الصيف يقول الحصادون، 'رأيناه يراقص
أوراق الخريف وفي شعره ندفة ثلج.'

قلتم كل ذلك عن الجمال، لكنكم لم تتحدثوا في
الحقيقة عنه، بل عن حاجات لم تشبع بعد.

ليس الجمال بحاجة. إن الجمال نشوة.

ليس الجمال ثغراً ظامئاً ولا يداً فارغة ممدودة إلى
أمام،

But rather a heart enflamed and a soul enchanted.

It is not the image you would see nor the song you would hear,

But rather an image you see though you close your eyes and a song you hear though you shut your ears.

It is not the sap within the furrowed bark, nor a wing attached to a claw,

But rather a garden forever in bloom and a flock of angles forever in flight.

People of Orphalese, beauty is life when life unveils her holy face.

But you are life and you are the veil.

Beauty is eternity gazing at itself in a mirror.

بل قلب تلظى وروح أسكرها الهيام.

ليس الجمال صورة ترونها ولا أغنية تسمعونها،

بل صورة ترونها وإن أغمضت العيون وأغنية

تسمعونها وإن صُمّت الآذان.

ليس الجمال نسغاً في لحاء متغضن، ولا جناحاً

موصولاً بمخلب،

بل سرب ملائكة دائم الطيران وبستان أبدي الريَعان.

يا أهل أورفليس، الجمال هو الحياة أماطت عن

وجهها الطهور اللثام.

لكنكم الحياة وأنتم اللثام.

الجمال هو الخلود يحدق بذاته في مرآة.

203

But you are eternity and you are the mirror.

لكنكم الخلود وأنتم المرآة.

AND an old priest said, Speak to us of
Religion.

And he said:

Have I spoken this day of aught else?

Is not religion all deeds and all reflection,

And that which is neither deed nor
reflection, but a wonder and a surprise ever
springing in the soul, even while the hands
hew the stone or tend the loom?

Who can separate his faith from his
actions, or his belief from his occupations?

Who can spread his hours before him,
saying, 'This for God and this for myself;
This for my soul, and this other for my
body?'

All your hours are wings that beat
through space from self to self.

وقال كاهن هرِم، حدثنا عن **الدين**،

فقال:

وهل تحدثت اليوم عن شيء آخر؟

أليس الدين الأعمال كل الأعمال، والاستذكار كل الاستذكار،

وما هو ليس بعمل ولا استذكار، بل عجَب ودهَش أبداً في الروح يفيضان،

حتى عندما في الحجر تنقش وبالنول تنسج اليدان؟

من يستطيع فصل إيمانه عن أفعاله، أو عقيدته عن أشغاله؟

من يستطيع بسط ساعاته أمامه، قائلاً، 'هذه لله وهذه لنفسي؛ هذه لروحي وهذه الأخرى لجسدي؟'

كل ساعاتكم أجنحة تضرِب في الفضاء من نفس لنفس.

He who wears his morality but as his best garment were better naked.

The wind and the sun will tear no holes in his skin.

And he who defines his conduct by ethics imprisons his song-bird in a cage.

The freest song comes not through bars and wires.

And he to whom worshipping is a window, to open but also to shut, has not yet visited the house of his soul whose windows are from dawn to dawn.

Your daily life is your temple and your religion.

Whenever you enter into it take with you your all.

من يلبس فضيلته كأحسن ثوب لديه، أحرى أن يكون بلا رداء.

فلا الشمس ستثقب لحمه ولا الهواء.

ومن يحدد سلوكه بمناقب الأدب يحبس طائره المغرد في قفص.

نشيد الحرية الأكبر لا يأتي عبر أسلاك وقضبان.

ومن كانت العبادة له نافذة، تفتح ومثلما تفتح تغلَق، لم يحل في مضارب روحه بعد، حيث النوافذ مشرعة من الفجر إلى الفجر.

حياتك اليومية دينك ومحرابك.

كلما دخلت المحراب خذ كل ما لك معك،

Take the plough and the forge and the mallet and the lute,

The things you have fashioned in necessity or for delight.

For in reverie you cannot rise above your achievements nor fall lower than your failures.

And take with you all men:

For in adoration you cannot fly higher than their hopes nor humble yourself lower than their despair.

And if you would know God, be not therefore a solver of riddles.

Rather look about you and you shall see Him playing with your children.

خذ العودَ والمحراث والمطرقة والكير،

ما صنعته لحاجة أو ما ابتدعته لسرور.

فلا أنت في أحلام يقظتك فوق مآثرك صاعد ولا دون

إخفاقك بالغ في الهبوط.

وخذ كل الرجال معك:

فلا أنت في هيامك فوق آمالهم محلق ولا دون يأسهم

مُدنٍ نفسك في القنوط.

وإن أردت أن تعرف الله، فلا تذهب في حل لغز.

تلفت بدلاً من ذلك حولك وستراه يلاعب أطفالك.

211

And look into space; you shall see Him walking in the cloud, outstretching His arms in the lightning and descending in rain.

You shall see Him smiling in flowers, then rising and waving his hands in trees.

وانظر في الفضاء؛ ستراه في الغمام، ذراعاه في البرق وجلاله في المطر.

وستراه باسماً في الزهر، ثم صاعداً يلوح يديه في الشجر.

THEN Almitra spoke, saying, We would ask now of **Death**.

And he said:

You would know the secret of death.

But how shall you find it unless you seek it in the heart of life?

The owl whose night-bound eyes are blind unto the day cannot unveil the mystery of light.

If you would indeed behold the spirit of death, open your heart wide unto the body of life.

For life and death are one, even as the river and the sea are one.

In the depth of your hopes and desires lies your silent knowledge of the beyond;

ثم تكلمت ألمطرا، وقالت، نريد أن نسأل الآن عن

الموت.

فقال،

تريدون أن تعرفوا سر الموت.

لكن كيف ستجدونه إن لم تتقصوه في قلب الحياة؟

طائر البوم عينه تبصر الليل ولا تبصر النهار غير

قادر على فك أحجية الضياء.

لو أردتم إبصار روح الموت حقاً، أشرعوا قلوبكم

لجسد الحياة.

فالحياة والموت واحد، مثلما النهر والبحر واحد.

في عميق آمالك وأشواقك يكمن علمك الصامت

بالغيب؛

And like seeds dreaming beneath the snow your heart dreams of spring.

Trust the dreams, for in them is hidden the gate to eternity.

Your fear of death is but the trembling of the shepherd when he stands before the king whose hand is to be laid upon him in honour.

Is the shepherd not joyful beneath his trembling, that he shall wear the mark of the king?

Yet is he not more mindful of his trembling?

For what is it to die but to stand naked in the wind and to melt into the sun?

وكالبذور الحالمة تحت غطاء الثلج يحلم قلبك بالربيع.

صدقي الأحلام، فإنها تخفي السبيل إلى الخلود.

ما خوفكم من الموت إلا ارتعاش راع أمام مليك ستلمسه يده بإكرام.

ألا يخفي الراعي تحت ارتعاشه فرحاً، لأنه سيحمل علامة الملك؟

أولا يفكر مع ذلك بارتعاشه أكثر مما يفكر بفرحه؟

وهل الموت إلا وقفة عراء في الريح وذوبان في الشمس؟

And what is it to cease breathing, but to free the breath from its restless tides, that it may rise and expand and seek God unencumbered?

Only when you drink from the river of silence shall you indeed sing.

And when you have reached the mountain top, then you shall begin to climb.

And when the earth shall claim your limbs, then shall you truly dance.

وهل توقف الأنفاس إلا خلاص من صريف مد وجزر
كي تصعد الأنفاس وتمتد، وتنشد الباري بلا عوق؟

لن تعرفوا الغناء حتى تترعوا من نهر السكون.
وعندما تبلغون قمة الجبل، ستبدأون للتو بالصعود.
وعندما تطالب الأرض بأوصالكم، سترقصون كما
يجدر بالرقص أن يكون.

And now it was evening.

And Almitra the seeress said, Blessed be this day and this place and your spirit that has spoken.

And he answered:

Was it I who spoke? Was I not also a listener?

Then he descended the steps of the temple and all the people followed him. And he reached his ship and stood upon the deck.

And facing the people again, he raised his voice and said:

People of Orphalese, the wind bids me leave you.

Less hasty am I than the wind, yet I must go.

وهنا حل المساء.

وقالت العرافة ألمطرا، بورك هذا النهار وهذا المكان وروحك التي تكلمت اليوم.

فأجاب:

هل أنا من تكلم؟ ألم أكن كذلك منصتاً للقول؟

ثم نزل درجات المعبد يتبعه الخلق فجاء السفينة فصعد متنها، فإذا ما واجه الناس ثانية، جهر بالصوت:

يا معشر أورفليس، الريح تدعوني لأغادركم.

إني أقل عجلة من الريح، لكن الرحيل علي حتم.

We wanderers, ever seeking the lonlier way, begin no day when we have ended another day; and no sunrise finds us where sunset left us.

Even while the earth sleeps we travel.

We are the seeds of the tenacious plant, and it is in our ripeness and our fullness of heart that we are given to the wind and are scattered.

Brief were my days among you, and briefer still the words I have spoken.

But should my voice fade in your ears, and my love vanish in your memory, then I will come again,

And with a richer heart and lips more yielding to the spirit will I speak.

Yea, I shall return with the tide,

نحن الهائمين، أبداً نبحث عن نائي الدروب، لا نبدأ
يوماً حيث أمضينا غيره، ولا يطالعنا شروق حيث غادرنا
غروب.

حتى والأرض نائمة نسير.

نحن بذور النبت العتيد، ما أن تتفتح قلوبنا ونصير
إلى نضوج حتى تأخذنا وتبعثرنا الريح.

كانت أيامي وجيزة بينكم، وأقل منها كلماتي لكم.

فإذا ما خبا صوتي في مسامعكم، وغاب حبي عن
تذكركم، فثانية سأعود،

وبقلب أكثر ثراء سأحدثكم، وبشفاه أكثر إحساساً
بالروح.

أجل، إني مع المد عائد،

And though death may hide me and the greater silence enfold me, yet again will I seek your understanding.

And not in vain will I seek.

If aught I have said is truth, that truth shall reveal itself in a clearer voice, and in words more kin to your thoughts.

I go with the wind, people of Orphalese, but not down into emptiness;

And if this day is not a fulfilment of your needs and my love, then let it be a promise till another day.

Man's needs change, but not his love, nor his desire that his love should satisfy his needs.

Know therefore, that from the greater silence I shall return.

قد يغيبني الموت ويطويني الصمت الأعظم، لكني سأظل أنشد فهمكم.

ولن تكون نَشدتي عبثاً.

فإذا كان مما قلت اليوم الحقيقة، فبصوت أكثر جلاء وكلمات أقرب إلى أفكاركم ستكشف عن ذاتها الحقيقة.

إني ذاهب مع الريح يا أهل أورفليس، ولن أهبط إلى فراغ؛

فإن لم يكن هذا اليوم رياً لحاجاتكم ولحبي لكم، فوعد إلى غير يوم.

تتغير الإنسان حاجاته، ولا يتغير حبه، ولا شوقه لأن يروي حبه حاجاته.

فاعلموا، أني من الصمت الأعظم عائد.

The mist that drifts away at dawn, leaving but dew in the fields, shall rise and gather into a cloud and then fall down in rain.

And not unlike the mist have I been.

In the stillness of the night I have walked in your streets, and my spirit has entered your houses,

And your heart-beats were in my heart, and your breath was upon my face, and I knew you all.

Ay, I knew your joy and your pain, and in your sleep your dreams were my dreams.

And oftentimes I was among you a lake among the mountains.

I mirrored the summits in you and the bending slopes, and even the passing flocks of your thoughts and desires.

قدر الضباب السابح في الفجر، مخلفاً الطل في الحقول، أن يصعد ويتجمع غمامة لا تلبث أن تصب.

ولم أكن غير ما كان الضباب.

في سكون الليل طفت شوارعكم، وانسلت روحي في منازلكم،

وجيبكم كان في قلبي وعلى وجهي سرَت أنفاسكم، وعرفت كل واحد فيكم.

إِيه، عرفت فرحكم وألمكم، وفي نومكم كانت أحلامكم أحلامي.

لطالما كنت بينكم بحيرة بين الجبال.

عكستُ ذراكم وتعرجَ منحدراتكم، وحتى خواطركم وأسراب وأشواقكم.

And to my silence came the laughter of your children in streams, and the longing of your youth in rivers.

And when they reached my depth the streams and the rivers ceased not yet to sing.

But sweeter still than laughter and greater than longing came to me.

It was the boundless in you;

The vast man in whom you are all but cells and sinews;

He in whose chants all your singing is but a soundless throbbing.

It is in the vast man that you are vast,

And in beholding him that I beheld you and loved you.

ضحكات أطفالكم جاءت صمتي جداول، وشوق شبابكم جاءه أنهراً.

هذي الجداول وهذي الأنهر ما برحت مذ لامست أعماقي في غناء.

لكنها أحلى من الضحك وصلت إلي، وأعظم من الشوق.

كان ذلك اللانهائي فيكم؛

الإنسان الأكبر الذي ما أنتم فيه إلا خلايا وأعصاب؛

الذي ما غناؤكم في نشيده إلا خفضات ألحان.

ما رحابكم إلا من رحاب ذلك الإنسان.

إذ رأيته رأيتكم وإذ رأيتكم أحببتكم.

For what distances can love reach that are not in that vast sphere?

What visions, what expectations and what presumptions can outsoar that flight?

Like a giant oak tree covered with apple blossoms is the vast man in you.

His might binds you to the earth, his fragrance lifts you into space, and in his durability you are deathless.

You have been told that, even like a chain, you are as weak as your weakest link.

This is but half the truth. You are also as strong as your strongest link.

To measure you by your smallest deed is to reckon the power of ocean by the frailty of its foam.

فأي مسافات يطولها الحب ولا تضمها تلك الرحاب؟

أي رؤى، أي آمال، وأي افتراضات تحلق فوق هاتيك الأبعاد؟

الإنسان الأكبر فيكم مثل شجرة سنديان سنيّة تكسوها براعم تفاح.

بالأرض يوثقكم جبروته، ويرفعكم عبيره إلى الفضاء، وفي بقائه تهزمون الموت.

قيل لكم إنكم كالسلسلة ضعفاء كأكثر حلقاتكم ضعفاً. إنما هذه نصف الحقيقة. فأنتم كذلك أقوياء كأشد حلقاتكم بأساً.

قياسكم بصغائر أعمالكم كقياس هول البحر بهشاشة الزبد.

To judge you by your failures is to cast blame upon the seasons for their inconstancy.

Ay, you are like an ocean,
And though heavy-grounded ships await the tide upon your shores, yet, even like an ocean, you cannot hasten your tides.
And like the seasons you are also,
And though in winter you deny your spring,
Yet spring, reposing within you, smiles in her drowsiness and is not offended.
Think not I say these things in order that you may say the one to the other, 'He praised us well. He saw but the good in us.'
I only speak to you in words of that which you yourselves know in thought.

والحكم عليكم من عثراتكم كلوم الفصول لتقلبها منذ
الأبد.

بلى، مثل محيط أنتم،

ورغم أن سفناً مثقلة تنتظر في مرافئكم المد، فأنتم،

كالبحر، لا تملكون استعجال مدكم.

وكالفصول أنتم،

ورغم أنكم في شتائكم تنكرون ربيعكم،

فالربيع الهاجع فيكم، يبتسم في رقاده ولا يستاء.

لا تحسبوا أني أقول هذا كي يقول أحدكم للآخر،

'لقد أحسن مدحنا. لم ير فينا إلا الخير.'

إنما أحدثكم بالكلام عما تدركونه بالقلب.

And what is word knowledge but a shadow of wordless knowledge?

Your thoughts and my words are waves from a sealed memory that keeps records of our yesterdays,

And of the ancient days when the earth knew not us nor herself,

And of nights when earth was upwrought with confusion.

Wise men have come to you to give you of their wisdom. I came to take of your wisdom:

And behold I have found that which is greater than wisdom.

وهل المعرفة بالقول إلا ظل معرفة بلا قول؟
أفكاركم وكلماتي أمواج ذاكرة خَتِمت، تحفظ لوح الأمس،
وغابر أيام لم تعرفنا حينها ولم تعرف نفسها الأرض،
وليال ماد فيها الكوكب وتولاه عصف.

بحكمتهم جاءكم حكماء. وجئت أنهل من حكمتكم:
فانظروا، أعظم من الحكمة وجدت.

It is a flame spirit in you ever gathering more of itself,

While you, heedless of its expansion, bewail the withering of your days,

It is life in quest of life in bodies that fear the grave.

There are no graves here.

These mountains and plains are a cradle and a stepping-stone.

Whenever you pass by the field where you have laid your ancestors look well thereupon, and you shall see yourselves and your children dancing hand in hand.

Verily you often make merry without knowing.

روحاً من لهيب فيكم أبداً يزداد من ذاته التهاباً، وأنتم، غافلون عن مده، تندبون زوال العمر، إنما هي الحياة تبحث عن حياة في أجساد تخشى القبر.

لا توجد قبور هنا.

هذي الجبال والسهول مهد ومعراج.

كلما مررتم بأرض وارت أسلافكم أمعنوا النظر، وسترون أنفسكم وأبناءكم ترقصون يداً بيد.

فلطالما هاجكم مرح وأنتم غافلون عن مرحكم.

Others have come to you to whom for golden promises made unto your faith you have given but riches and power and glory.

Less than a promise have I given, and yet more generous have you been to me.

You have given me my deeper thirsting after life.

Surely there is no greater gift to a man than that which turns all his aims into parching lips and all life into a fountain.

And in this lies my honour and my reward,-

That whenever I come to the fountain to drink I find the living water itself thirsty;

And it drinks me while I drink it.

Some of you have deemed me proud and over-shy to receive gifts.

وجاءكم آخرون بوعود براقة خاطبت إيمانكم فأغدقتم عليهم وما أغدقتم إلا المال والسلطان والمجد.

أقل من وعد قدمت، ورغم هذا كنتم معي أكثر كرماً.

منحتموني عطشي الأعمق للحياة.

ليس أعظم للإنسان من هبة تحيل غاياته ظمأ والحياة ينبوع ماء.

وفي هذا جزائي ومكرمتي،–

أن أرِد النبع شارباً فأجد ذات الماء الحي عطشان؛ وفيما أشرب الماء يشربني الماء.

بعضكم حسبني متعففاً يمنعني عن قبول العطايا حياء.

Too proud indeed am I to receive wages, but not gifts.

And though I have eaten berries among the hills when you would have me sit at your board,

And slept in the portico of the temple when you would gladly have sheltered me,

Yet was it not your loving mindfulness of my days and my nights that made food sweet to my mouth and girdled my sleep with visions?

For this I bless you most:

You give much and know not that you give at all.

Verily the kindness that gazes upon itself in a mirror turns to stone.

شديد التعفف عن تلقي الأجور أنا، ولكن ليس عن تلقي العطاء.

ورغم أني بين التلال التوت أكلت وكنتم ستقدمون لي على موائدكم الغذاء،

وفي رواق المعبد نمت وكنتم ستقدمون ليَ الملجأ والغطاء،

أولم يكن حنوكم على أيامي ولیالي ما ملأ نومي مع ذلك بالرؤى وجعل طعامي حلو المذاق؟

أكثر ما أباركككم لأنكم:

بسخاء تعطون ولا تدرون لعطائكم عطاء.

تستحيل اللطافة تحدق بذاتها في مرآة حجراً لا مراء،

And a good deed that calls itself by tender names becomes the parent to a curse.

And some of you have called me aloof, and drunk with my own aloneness,

And you have said, 'He holds council with the trees of the forest, but not with men.

He sits alone on hill-tops and looks down upon our city.'

True it is that I have climbed the hills and walked in remote places.

How could I have seen you save from a great height or a great distance?

How can one be indeed near unless he be far?

وأبا لعنة يصبح صالح الأعمال إذا ما على ذاته خلع
بديع الأسماء .

وبعضكم قال إني ناء بنفسي، وبعزلتي سكران،
وقلتم، 'يجالس أشجار الغابة، ولا يجالس الرجال.
وحيداً يجلس ومدينتنا يرمق من على رؤوس التلال.'
صعدت التلال حقاً ورمت أبعد مكان.
وهل كان لي أن أراكم إلا من علو عظيم أو مسافة
عظيمة؟
كيف يكون المرء قريباً ما لم يكن بعيدا؟

And others among you called unto me, not in words, and they said,

'Stranger, stranger, lover of unreachable heights, why dwell you among the summits where eagles build their nests?

'Why seek you the unattainable?

'What storms would you trap in your net?

'And what vaporous birds do you hunt in the sky?

'Come and be one of us.

'Descend and appease your hunger with our bread and quench your thirst with our wine.'

In the solitude of their souls they said these things;

وناداني آخرون بينكم بلا كلام، قائلين،

'يا غريباً، يا أيها الغريب، يا عاشق ذرى المحال، لم

عيشك في الأعالي سكنى النسور؟

'لم بحثك عما لا يطال؟

'أي عواصف توْقِع في شرَكك،

'أي طيور من وهم تصيد في السماء؟

'تعال كن واحداً منا، هيا تعال.

'انزل دارِ جوعك بخبزنا وبنبيذنا أطفئ ظمأك.'

قالوا ذلك في عزلة روحهم؛

But were their solitude deeper they would have known that I sought but the secret of your joy and your pain,

And I hunted only your larger selves that walk the sky.

But the hunter was also the hunted;

For many of my arrows left my bow only to seek my own breast.

And the flier was also the creeper;

For when my wings were spread in the sun their shadow upon the earth was a turtle.

And I the believer was also the doubter;

For often have I put my finger in my own wound that I might have the greater belief in you and the greater knowledge of you.

ولو كانت عزلتهم أعمق لعلموا أني ما بحثت إلا عن سر فرحكم وسر ألمكم، وأني ما صدت إلا ذواتكم الأكبر في السماء.

لكن الصائد كان المصيد؛

فلم يغادر عديد سهامي قوسي إلا ليصيب صدري.

والطائر كان الزاحف في آن؛

فلما بسطت جناحي في الشمس كان ظلهما على الأرض سُلَحفاة.

وأنا المصدق كنت كذلك الشاك؛

فلكم أوغلت إصبعي بجرحي لأكون أكثر إيماناً ومعرفة بكم.

And it is with this belief and this knowledge that I say,

You are not enclosed within your bodies, nor confined to houses or fields.

That which is you dwells above the mountain and roves with the wind.

It is not a thing that crawls into the sun for warmth or digs holes into darkness for safety,

But a thing free, a spirit that envelops the earth and moves in the ether.

If these be vague words, then seek not to clear them.

Vague and nebulous is the beginning of all things, but not their end,

And I fain would have you remember me as a beginning.

بهذا الإيمان وهذه المعرفة أقول،

لن تطوقكم أجسادكم، ولن تحدكم بيوت أو حقول.

هذا الذي هو أنتم يسكن الجبال ومع الريح يجول.

هو ليس شيئاً يزحف نحو الشمس للدفء أو للأمان

يحفر في الظلام الجحور،

بل شيء من العتق، روح يغلف الأرض وفي الأثير

يمور.

إذا كانت هذي، كلماتي، غامضة، فلا تحاولوا جلو

الغموض.

غامضة سديمية بداية الأشياء، لا نهايتها.

ويا ليتكم تذكروني بداية إذ تتذكرون.

Life and all that lives, is conceived in the mist and not in the crystal.

And who knows but a crystal is mist in decay?

This would I have you remember in remembering me:

That which seems most feeble and bewildered in you is the strongest and most determined.

Is it not your breath that erected and hardened the structure of your bones?

And is it not a dream which none of you remember having dreamt, that builded your city and fashioned all there is in it?

Could you but see the tides of that breath you would cease to see all else,

And if you could hear the whispering of the dream you would hear no other sound.

الحياة وكل ما على الأرض يمور تشكل في الضبابي لا في الجلي.

ومن يعلم أن الجلي ضباب نحُل وصار إلى ظهور؟

وإذ تتذكرونني، هذا ما أتمنى أن تتذكروه:

أن ما يبدو أكثر ضعفاً فيكم وتحيراً هو الأقوى والأكثر عزماً.

فهل غير أنفاسكم ما أقام صلبكم وأعطاه الصلابة؟

أوليس حلماً لا يتذكره أحد ما بنى مدينتكم وصاغ ما فيها؟

لو استطعتم إبصار مد وجزر الأنفاس لما نظرتم لشيء غيره،

ولو استطعتم سماع همس الحلم لما أصغيتم لصوت غيره.

But you do not see, nor do you hear, and it is well.

The veil that clouds your eyes shall be lifted by the hands that wove it,

And the clay that fills your ears shall be pierced by those fingers that kneaded it.

And you shall see

And you shall hear.

Yet you shall not deplore having known blindness, nor regret having been deaf.

For in that day you shall know the hidden purposes in all things,

And you shall bless darkness as you would bless light.

لكنكم لا تبصرون، ولكنكم لا تسمعون، وذلك خير.

الحجاب الذي يغشي أبصاركم سترفعه اليد التي نسجته،
والطين الذي يقر آذانكم ستثقبه الأصابع التي
عجنته.

ولسوف تبصرون

ولسوف تسمعون.

ولن يضيركم أنكم عرفتم العمى، ولن يحزنكم أنكم
عرفتم الصمم.

فيومئذ ستدركون الغايات الخافية في الأشياء.

وستباركون الظلام مثلما تباركون الضياء.

After saying these things he looked about him, and he saw the pilot of his ship standing by the helm and gazing now at the full sails and now at the distance.

And he said:

Patient, over patient, is the captain of my ship.

The wind blows and restless are the sails;

Even the rudder begs direction;

Yet quietly my captain awaits my silence.

And these my mariners, who have heard the choir of the greater sea, they too have heard me patiently.

Now they shall wait no longer.

I am ready.

The stream has reached the sea, and once more the great mother holds her son against her breast.

قال ذلك وتلفت حوله، فرأى ربان سفينته واقفاً حد الدفة يرنو تارة إلى المدى وتارة إلى الشراع.

ثم قال:

طال الصبر بربان سفينتي.

الريح تعصف والشراع في اضطراب؛

حتى الدفة تلتمس اتجاهاً؛

رغم هذا، رباني ينتظر صمتي.

وهؤلاء، بحارتي الذين سمعوا تراتيل البحر الأعظم،

أصغوا بصبر كذلك لي.

ولن ينتظروا أكثر.

إني مستعد.

بلغ الجدول البحر، والأم العظيمة تأخذ ابنها إلى صدرها من جديد.

Fare you well, people of Orphalese.

This day had ended.

It is closing upon us even as the water-lily upon its own tomorrow.

What was given us here we shall keep,

And if it suffices not, then again must we come together and together stretch our hand unto the giver.

Forget not that I shall come back to you.

A little while, and my longing shall gather dust and foam for another body.

A little while, a moment of rest upon the wind, and another woman shall bear me.

Farewell to you and the youth I have spent with you.

It was but yesterday we met in a dream.

وداعاً، يا أهل أورفليس.

لقد أدبر النهار.

إنه يطبق علينا كما على غده زنبق الماء.

قد نابنا هاهنا جزاء ولسوف نحفظ هذا الجزاء،

وإن لم يكن ما أوتيناه اليوم كافياً، فثانية سنلتقي ونمد

أيدينا لصاحب العطاء.

لا تنسوا أني عائد.

هنيهة، ويكسو شوقي زبد وغبار لجسد آخر.

هنيهة، لحظة راحة على جناح الريح، ويحملني رحم

آخر.

وداعاً لكم ولشباب أمضيته معكم.

قد جمعَنا بالأمس حلم.

You have sung to me in my aloneness, and I of your longings have built a tower in the sky.

But now our sleep has fled and our dream is over, and it is no longer dawn.

The noontide is upon us and our half waking has turned to fuller day, and we must part.

If in the twilight of memory we should meet once more, we shall speak again together and you shall sing to me a deeper song.

And if our hands should meet in another dream, we shall build another tower in the sky.

ولقد شدوتم لي في وحدتي، ومن أشواقكم بنيت برجاً في السماء.

والآن طار نومنا وتلاشى حلمنا، وتوارى الفجر.

مد الظهيرة علا ونصف يقظتنا أوغل في النهار، وحان الفراق.

إذا ما في غسق الذاكرة التقينا، فثانية سنتكلم وستنشدون لي أغنية أعمق.

وإذا ما تصافحت أيدينا بحلم آخر، فبرجاً آخر سنبني في السماء.

So saying he made signal to the seamen, and straightway they weighed anchor and cast the ship loose from its moorings, and they moved eastward.

And a cry came from the people as from a single heart, and it rose into the dusk and was carried out over the sea like a great trumpeting.

Only Almitra was silent, gazing unto the ship until it had vanished into the mist.

And when all the people were dispersed she still stood alone upon the sea-wall, remembering in her heart his saying:

'A little while, a moment of rest upon the wind, and another woman shall bear me.'

قال ذلك وأومأ للبحارة، فكالوا المرساة وحرروا السفينة من حبالها، ويمموا شطر الشرق.

وإذا بصيحة يطلقها الخلق كأنما من صميم واحد، صعدت حواشي الشفق من على أديم الماء وكالبوق الهادر جابت الأرجاء.

وحدها ألمطرا بقيت صامتة، تشيع السفينة حتى غيبها الضباب.

وإذ تفرق القوم جميعاً ظلت واقفة وحدها على سور البحر، وفي قلبها تتذكر قوله،

'هنيهة، لحظة راحة على جناح الريح، ويحملني رحم آخر.'

النبي

(هذا الكتاب يقرأ من اليسار)

الفهرس

إلى كاترينا ورايان.

تقديم

من قرأ النبي ولم تعصف برأسه ريح قادمة من الغيب، ولم تغمض الرؤى جفنيه بالنشوة ألف مرة، ولم يصعد به الخيال إلى المحال، لم يقرأه في الحقيقة.

قارئ نبي جبران قارئ متأمل ينفذ إلى الأبعاد. تشغله قضية الروح، والحب والسلام.

هو قارئ قادر على اقتناص الرؤى التي خطت الكتاب؛ رؤى شفّت لإحساس جبران المبصر كما تشف في إناء البلور الأسماك.

وكيف يتحقق ذلك ما لم يكن القارئ ميالاً بالفطرة للإبحار في الآفاق؟

هناك القريب وهناك البعيد. وهناك الأقرب وهناك الأبعد. تتعدد المسافات وهي ليست بمسافات، بل ذكريات. كل شيء يسكن في كل شيء، وكل شيء يدرك في الصمت كل شيء. هناك من يقول عن جبران إنه عصي على الفهم. وهناك من يقول إنه بحجم الحياة. هناك من يقرأ جبران أفكاراً على صفحات كتاب. وهناك من يقرأه إحساساً في الذات.

مثلما فطرت الطبيعة الأفراد على الإبحار في الخيال، وعلى التجوال الساهي بين المجرات، وعلى السمر مع النجوم في الليالي الصافيات، وعلى التقلب على أرائك الضباب في ثنايا الأحلام، فطرت جبران على السفر في الغيب وجهزته بالمجسات.

لا حدود هناك للتفاعل بين الطبيعة والإنسان، وللتبصر والاكتشاف والإلهام. يلهم الله من يشاء. ويمنح من يشاء الوسائل والغايات.

جبران حالة شفافية وإبصار. تعلق بالطبيعة وفهم روح الجمال. وهو حالة إيمان بالغيب أيضاً.

يخطئ من يظن أن أفكار ورؤى جبران شطحات خيال. لا تأخذ الرؤى والأفكار شاعراً بلا نداء.

السماء بعيدة والبعد درب والدروب وصال.

أعلى الأغصان يربطها مع أدناها درب، وأكبر النجوم يربطها مع أصغر الأقمار وثاق.

ما نأى بالمسافة دنا بالتأمل والاستبصار، وما وارته الحجب قربه الخيال. التأمل والخيال جناحان لا يهابان المسافات. كاسران عملاقان لهما عش في

ii

الأكوان، أوجدهما الذي أوجد الخلق وجعلهما مرسالاً بين الإنسان والأبراج؛ جوادان صهوتهما الإحساس وعنانهما الأحلام.

ليست الحقيقة التي بحث عنها جبران رمزاً يفسَر أو شيفرة تفَك، بل وجوداً في كل وجود، بذرة في كل بذرة، رؤية في كل رؤية، نسيماً يلثم روح الأشياء.

كتب جبران من وحي إصغائه وتأمله الأعمق، لا من عصارة قراءاته وخلاصة دراساته. إحساسه كان صهوته. ولسوف يأتي يوم نسمع فيه ما سمعه ونرى ما رآه؛ عندما نزداد توغلاً في الطبيعة واستغراقاً في كنه الحياة، كما فعل جبران.

لا يحس بنشوة الغمامة الحزينة في ترحالها الخصيب إلا بصير القلب والإحساس. قدر الإنسان الذي انطلق من الكهوف إلى الرخاء أن يجول في الملكوت بالخيال.

النبي بوصلة تشير إلى مساكن الروح؛ حالة شفافية ونفاذ يتضاءل أمامها كل الشعر. كل الذين يحجون إلى مرقد جبران اللبناني من أطراف الأرض يؤمنون بحقيقة الروح ويسحرهم إبداعه في رسمها وحديثه عنها. في بُشَرّي، في أحشاء الصخور المطلة على وادي قاديشا المقدس، حيث أفرغ أحزانه طفلاً وأصغى في الأصائل للصمت الكبير؛ حيث تسفح أشعة الشمس الغاربة

الصخور برقة وفتنة وجلال، هناك، في كهف صغير بين تلك الصخور، يرقد جبران جسداً فانياً وروحاً حية. يذهب الجسد وتبقى الروح على مر الزمان.

ثمة من فهم جبران كل الفهم، ومن فهمه نصف الفهم، ومن هو في الطريق إلى فهمه، ومن لم يستطع معه فهماً. لكن غموض جبران بعض من غموض الحياة. يقول في *النبي*:

"*إذا كانت هذي، كلماتي، غامضة، فلا تحاولوا جلو الغموض.*
غامضة سديمية بداية الأشياء، لا نهايتها.
ويا ليتكم تتذكروني بداية إذ تتذكرون.
الحياة وكل ما على الأرض يمور تشكل في الضبابي لا في الجلي.
ومن يعلم أن الجلي ضباب نحل وصار إلى ظهور؟"

طور الإنسان علومه التجريبية بنجاح لكن معرفته الروحية قصرت عن المواكبة. غير أن الطبيعة تتكفل بنمو الوعي بالروح كما يتكفل التراب بالسنبلة. تُطور الطبيعة الإبداعَ في الإنسان. تكثف نسغ الموهبة. تزيد حدة الإحساس وتعمق الرؤية. تنقي عدسة الجمال وترهف الأسماع. تؤجج حب الاكتشاف.

النبي سِفر يتكلم بين دفتيه الصمت وتحكي حكايتها الأكوان؛ دفق فكري يختزل حكاية الخلق. من يفهم عجينة نهاد حداد، ونقاوة جانيت فغالي،

وكهوف الصدى التي جاء منها وديع فرانسيس يستطيع السير في إثر جبران، فهؤلاء وأمثالهم وجبران من نبع واحد سخرته الطبيعة لسقيا الروح والارتقاء بخيال وذائقة الإنسان.

جبران نهر إحساس مبصر وألق كلمات. حالة إبصار تذوب أمام مدها الأميال. حبكة مثلى تروي قصة الإنسان. قصيدة تغني الفرح. دمعة تختصر الأحزان.

اللحظة التي أطلقت العنان لخيال جبران كانت لحظة حزن وفرح معاً. ما بدا في قلبه حزناً تحول إلى فرح في آن، لتصيبه دهشة من وحدة الأضداد في الحياة أثارت حفيظته وعمقت رؤاه. بالحزن والألم تتسع مساحة الحب في القلب. يكبر الفؤاد. تتصافح تحت القبة الزرقاء الأصوات. تتصالح العناصر في الوجدان. يقول في النبي:

"ألمكم هو انكسار القوقعة التي تطوق فهمكم.
وكما على نواة الثمرة أن تنفلق ليشرئب لبها في الشمس، عليكم اختبار الألم.
"ولو استطعتم إبقاء قلوبكم في دهش أمام معجزات حياتكم تتبدى كل يوم، لأمنتم إلى أن ألمكم لا يقل دهشاً عن فرحكم؛
ولقبلتم بمواسم قلوبكم قبولكم تعاقب الفصول على حقولكم.
ولرقبتم بهدوء وصفو تعاقب شتاء حزنكم."

٧

كاشف الألم لا يضاهيه مصباح. ليس مثل شمعة الحزن ما يشيع نور الفرح. يتفشى الألم في الفرح كما يتفشى الحبر في النشاف. وينسرب الفرح في الألم كما ينسرب الفجر في الظلام.

شذب الألم نفس جبران كما تشذب الأصابع المبدعة الأغصان. لم تفرح كلماته بلا حزن ولم تحزن بلا فرح. امتزج فرحه بألمه امتزاج الشعاع بالرذاذ. بالتأمل وبعين الإحساس وبالخيال اكتشف جبران وحدة في الكون والحياة، وقبل بالحزن قبوله بالفرح. لم يسحقه الحزن كما يسحق غيره. لم يجرفه إلى حفر اليأس والتسليم والعذاب. لقد رأى حكمة العلي في الأشياء.

عندما في القلب والعقل يطل سؤال، تتفتح نوافذ الأسرار، ويتنفس في الرؤى جواب. أدب جبران بيان حول حال الحياة زاده إبداعه اللغوي سطراً؛ بذرة متطورة الخصائص من بذور الأفكار. ولسوف تتوالى البذور المبدعة في الأرحام، حتى بزوغ شمس *اليوم الثاني في الحياة* من رحم الضباب.

جبران وعدٌ حين عز الوعد. بصيص نور من الغيب. أغنية يتمايل لجرسها القلب وتطرب الآذان. سِفر إيمان بحقيقة الروح. سفينة نوح. عين على المعجزات. حبل نجاة من سأم الأيام.

نقل جبران الأدب من حكايات الصراع والاقتتال والحب المقنن والافتتان بالمادة والهزائم والبطولات إلى حكاية أكبر من كل الحكايات؛ حكاية الغيب والأحلام والغايات.

من سخريات القدر أن الراهن- على صغره وضآلته، يطغى في الوعي على الأزلي اللامتناه. في الراهن إلحاحية جوع وشبع واكتفاء، وفي الأزلي روح يعرف سر الليالي والأيام.

المتأملون تستيقظ روحهم قبل غيرهم. تشف لبصيرتهم صور وراء الصور وتشنَّف أسماعُهم لأصوات وراء الأصوات. هم رواد الحقيقة الذين يرون التشابهات ويعقدون المقارنات. لا يعرف الإنسان السر، أجل، لكنه لا ينكر السر. وبين القلب والعقل مسافات تنتظر أن تقطع.

جاء جبران بحديث عن الغيب إثباته يكمن في عدم إنكاره وعدم إنكاره إقرار أبكم به. عندما طحن الألم قلبه على ضفاف *قاديشا* ورافقه في البحار ثم في أزقة بوسطن ومجازات نيويورك، كان الخيال وحده ملاذه. لم يكتب سِفره لنقرأه ونتغنى به، ولا لنشربه ونثمل بخمرته، ولا لتزداد معارفنا بمحتواه. كتبه ليوقظ فينا الروح، ليسمو بالإنسان إلى ذرى ذاته الأكبر، وليحيده عن دروب ذاته القزم.

لم يشأ جبران أن يقدم نفسه ناصحاً أو معلماً. تكلم وكان مصغياً في ذات الوقت للقول. يصغي المتكلم لكلامه عندما يكون كلامه إملاء وحي وإلهاماً من الطبيعة بينما يمضي على دروب الكشف الذي يسبق الفهم.

ماذا لو كانت الحقيقة الكلية جلية من البدء؟ ماذا لو كانت صفحة نقرأها في كتاب؟ أليس ما يشد الجنس للجنس الآخر هو ما يختزنه هذا الآخر من فيض؟ أليس البحث عن السر أكثر سحراً من السر؟ أليس الغموض أصل الفضول؟ ألا تتوقف الحياة إذا ما جأرت خبايا الحياة؟ أليس أعظم القول هو ما لم يقل بعد؟ أليس العطش عطاء مثلما الارتواء عطاء؟ وما قيمة الارتواء إن لم يسبقه ظمأ؟

ينشغل الإنسان اليوم بكل شيء إلا الروح التي تحدث عنها جبران. لكن، ألا تخدش رعونة الإنسان اليوم حياء الشمس؟ ألا يسير على طريق الجريمة والدم؟ ألا يفسد في الأرض؟ ألا يلوث الهواء والماء؟ ألا يسمم الأديم ويذبح الأطفال ويغتصب العذارى ويعمَه في الشر؟ ألا يشيع التشاؤم والإحباط؟ ألا يحطم الآمال؟ ألا يسجن الأحلام؟ ألا يزيد زنازين التسلط والقهر؟ ألا ينشر الأنانية والمزيد القادم منها؟ ألا ينشر الجشع والمزيد القادم منه؟ ألا ينشر الاكتئاب والمزيد القادم منه؟ ألا ينشر الدمار والمزيد القادم منه؟

من سيوقف عويل الثكالى؟ من سينقذ الأطفال أولاً من الآباء؟ من سيمنع البرد عن اللحم الطري؟ من سيصغي لشكوى الحيوان؟ من سيكتشف أحلام الطير؟ من سيستلهم قيم الجمال؟ من سيزرع النشوة في كل قلب؟ من سيجعل الثقافة قانون حياة؟ من سيحمي كبرياء الأوتار؟ من سيحيّ على الصلاة مع البحيرات والجبال والغابات؟ من سيغني للأزل تراتيل العرفان؟

أخطأ الإنسان الدرب إذ نسي الروح وتمادى في طعن عذرية الأرض. لكن جبران رفع الراية البيضاء بلا لوم بعدما دحر الشر في نفسه والتمس ذات الفعل من الإنسان. يقول في حديقة النبي:

"أن يسرقك الآخر، ويغشك ويخدعك، بلى، ويضللك ويتهكم ويتربص بك ويحيك لك الدوائر فتنتظر من علياء ذاتك الأكبر مبتسماً رغم ذلك ومدركاً أن ربيعاً في بستانك سيحل ويرقص في أوراقك، وأن خريفاً سيأتي لينضِج عنبك؛ وأن نافذة واحدة من نوافذك مشرعة على الشرق ستنأى بك إلى الأبد عن فراغك؛ وأن كل الذين احتُسِبوا لصوصاً وخطائين، وأهل خداع وغش، إخوة لك في ضيق، وأنك ربما كنت كل هؤلاء بعين المباركين، أهل مدينة الغيب التي فوق هذه المدينة."

عندما ينسى الإنسان حليبه الأول والأعماق والأفياء التي منها جاء، يقف في الشمس غصناً جافاً بلا تأمل يأتي بإلهام. تذروه الريح وتضنيه الأنواء. تمر الفصول من أمامه وهو لا يدري معنى لها، فهو في خواء يحيطه خواء.

مغلوب لا يدري بغلبه. معذب لا يعي عذابه. الإبداع من حوله ولا يرى الإبداع. المعجزات من حوله ولا يرى المعجزات.

ارتباط الإنسان بالطبيعة واستلهامها والتماهي بها احتماء بكنف الجلال. بقاء في الأول والآخر. تماحك مع الأزل؛ مع اللازمان واللامكان. فيه قوته وضعفه. وفيه مجده وذله. التلامس مع الطبيعة يتحول إلى تفاعل معها والتفاعل يؤدي إلى التأمل والتأمل إلى الإلهام، والإلهام لحظة إبداع.

من لا يروم آفاق الحياة يبقى غريباً على الحياة. لم تمنحنا الطبيعة الإحساس والخيال والإلهام صدفة. منحتنا كي نعيش الفصول مثلما عاشها جبران، وكي نتجول بين مساكن الروح مثلما تجول جبران، وكي نحب الإنسان الأكبر فينا مثلما أحبه جبران.

النبي مخاض روح الإنسان.

لكل ولادة مخاض.

للجسد مخاض.

وللروح مخاض.

جميل العابد

الطبعة الذهبية

عشرون عاماً مضت وأنا أشتغل على ترجمتي لنبي جبران؛ منذ الطبعة الأولى التي صدرت عام 1998 وحتى هذه الطبعة الثامنة التي تتوج كل ما سبقها من طبعات وتلغيها، فلن يكون هناك أي نسخة معدلة بعدها.

سوف يحكم القراء على ما إذا كانت هذه النسخة الذهبية من ترجمتي تطابق النص الأصل أفقاً وروحاً وإيقاعاً.

لقد كنت طوال اشتغالي على ترجمة رائعة جبران مدركاً أن المترجم قد ينفد بريشه في هنّات يقع فيها هنا أو هناك في ترجمته لأي كتاب، لكنه لن ينفد بريشه بأي حال عندما يكون النص المترجم *نبي جبران*.

سوف يحكم القراء على عملي الآن وفي قادم الزمان. ولسوف يكفيني أن يقال إني تصديت لأصعب المهام: ترجمةَ كاتب أكبر من كل الكتّاب، كاتب كتَب ليوقظ روح الإنسان.

مع المحبة،

جميل

هذه الترجمة تدهش وتفتن وتشغف. جريدة السفير اللبنانية.

هذا العمل الأنيق يكشف عن سعة علم المترجم، وهو تحد ينم عن قوته وثقته. د. رياض نور الله،
أستاذ الترجمة في جامعة وستمنستر، لندن

نقلت هذه الترجمة عذوبة الروح الجبرانية وشفافيته اوهو أمر افتقدناه في كل الترجمات السابقة
للكتاب. ولو أن جبران كتب النبي بالعربية فما كان ليكتبه إلا كما فعل جميل العابد بقلمه البارع.
د. صباح قباني، الأديب والإعلامي والدبلوماسي السوري.

شعرت وأنا أقارن هذه الترجمة بأنها الأصل وبأن الأصل هو الترجمة، كما رأيت أنها التقطت الظلال
الأبعد التي قصدها جبران ولم تسعفه اللغة التي كتب بها لإظهارها. د. زهير سمهوري، أستاذ فقه اللغة
الإنكليزية، جامعة دمشق.

نقف أمام قامتين، جبران وجميل، ونحار من منهما كتب النص بالعربية ومن كتبه بالإنكليزية. د.
محمد قجة، رئيس جمعية العاديات في سوريا، والأمين العام لاحتفالية حلب عاصمة للثقافة الإسلامية.

هذه الترجمة سلم علوي إلى الغيوم ونوافذ مشرعة نحو النجوم أتمنى أن أراها ملحنة ومغناة لأن كل
كلمة فيها تشع بالموسيقى والغناء وتوقظ الروح. د. رفيق الصبان، كاتب ومخرج النصوص التلفزيونية
والسينمائية.

يتساءل القارئ ما إذا كان هذا النص ترجمة أم أنه وضع في لغة الضاد ابتداءً. فاضل السباعي،
الروائي السوري.

حافظت هذه الترجمة على الوهج الذي نعرفه في رؤى جبران وصانت قوة تأثيرها ونزعتها إلى
الإبداع. حنا مينه، الروائي السوري.

أعود إلى النبي في ترجمة جميل العابد لأجده أبهى وأعمق مما أحفظ من ذكريات عن قراءاته
القديمة. د. عبد السلام العجيلي، الأديب والطبيب والبرلماني السوري.

الصور هنا أكثر دقة وذهنية وكثافة من النص الجبراني العادي. نحن أمام مترجم فذ لنص استثنائي
غير الأدب العالمي. د. بطرس حلاق، أستاذ الأدب العربي في جامعة السوربون، باريس، فرنسا.

هذا العمل الراقي يؤكد القدرة على نقل أهم الآثار الأدبية والفكرية والعلمية من اللغات الأجنبية إلى
اللغة العربية بدون أن تخسر شيئاً من معدنها الأصلي، ومن قيمتها وميزاتها الأساسية." د. رغيد
الصلح، جامعة أوكسفورد، إنكلترا.

الطبعة الثامنة (النسخة الذهبية)

حقوق جميل العابد كمؤلف لهذه الترجمة محفوظة وفقاً لحقوق النشر، والتصاميم وبراءات الاختراع التي نص عليها قانون 1988.

التقيم الدولي لطبعة الغلاف المقوى، والغلاف الورقي، والطبعة الالكترونية، كما يلي:

غلاف المقوى   ISBN: 978-0-9928995-2-3 (Paperback)

غلاف الورقي   978-0-9928995-3-0 (Hardback)

نسخة الكترونية   978-0-9928995-4-7 (ePub)

فهرس المكتبة البريطانية

العمل الفني للغلاف: **غلين د. وبستر**

النبي

جبران خليل جبران

إنكليزي - عربي

نقله

جميل العابد